STUDIES IN HISTORY, ECONOMICS AND PUBLIC LAW

EDITED BY THE FACULTY OF POLITICAL SCIENCE
OF COLUMBIA UNIVERSITY

Number 339

THE HISTORICAL BACKGROUNDS OF EARLY METHODIST ENTHUSIASM

THE HISTORICAL BACKGROUNDS OF EARLY METHODIST ENTHUSIASM

BY
UMPHREY LEE

AMS PRESS, INC.
NEW YORK
1967

AMS PRESS, INC.
New York, N.Y. 10003
1967

Oskar Diethelm Historical Library

Manufactured in the United States of America

In Memory
OF
MY FATHER

PREFACE

In the preparation of this slight volume I have been aided by scholars in this country and in England, and not least among these have been librarians who have allowed me to make use of their seventeenth and eighteenth century collections. Dr. Charles R. Gillett of Union Seminary has just edited a *Catalogue of the McAlpin Collection of British History and Theology,* which reveals the magnitude of the work done by the collectors of this library. It was in this collection that most of the source material for this study was found. In addition I must mention the libraries of Columbia University, the British Museum, the General Theological Seminary, Drew Theological Seminary, the University of Texas and Southern Methodist University.

Professor Lynn Thorndike of Columbia University has been good enough to make some very helpful criticisms. At the beginning of my work, Professor Reginald Harvey Griffith of the University of Texas pointed out to me the worth of studies in the history of ideas and introduced me to the literature of seventeenth and eighteenth century England. The Wrenn and Aitken Collections of that University have furnished much material for this volume.

But most of all I am under obligation to Professor William Walker Rockwell, now Librarian of Union Theological Seminary, under whose guidance this study has been carried out. Several years ago, he recommended to me the study of Methodist " enthusiasm "; and at his suggestion I undertook the preparation of a dissertation on the subject. To him I am indebted for more than academic guidance.

U. L.

Southern Methodist University.

TABLE OF CONTENTS

	PAGE
PREFACE	7
INTRODUCTION	11

CHAPTER I
Enthusiasm in Western Christendom to the Seventeenth Century. 13

CHAPTER II
English Enthusiasm from the Times of the Westminster Assembly to those of the Methodist Movement 38

CHAPTER III
Theological Controversies. 58

CHAPTER IV
"Philosophy" and Enthusiasm 76

CHAPTER V
Public Opinion of Enthusiasm. 98

CHAPTER VI
Methodist Enthusiasm	120
BIBLIOGRAPHY	149
INDEX	173

INTRODUCTION

THIS study of the backgrounds of Methodist enthusiasm is offered as an essay toward the better understanding of the Wesleyan movement. A chapter in the history of a single idea, such a study cannot explain so widespread and so influential a movement as that inaugurated by the Wesleys; but there are good reasons why enthusiasm offers a clue to the solution of certain difficulties in the history of Methodism.

Even a casual reader of Methodist history must remark the frequent charges of enthusiasm in the sense of a claim to be inspired directly by God himself, brought against the Wesleys and their followers. So vehement were the accusers and so concerned were the Methodists in denial that one cannot dismiss the disputes with vague references to the decorum of Georgian churchmen. Only an understanding of the connotations of " enthusiasm " in the minds of seventeenth and eighteenth century Englishmen will explain much of the opposition to the Wesleyan Revival. The history of the idea in the period, roughly a century, immediately preceding Methodism offers also some reasons for the rapid growth of the new societies in the face of determined opposition. Finally, by studying an idea instead of churches or sects, one may be the better able to place the Methodist Movement in the Christian tradition.

It should be kept in mind that this is not a study in the psychology of religion. The present interest is in the history of an idea: in its treatment by theologians and by philosophers, in evidences of the idea in popular opinion, in modifications and adaptations, and finally in the idea as it appears in Methodism. To make the story clear, the first chapter sketches the history of enthusiasm in Western Christendom up to the seventeenth century. Then, the story of enthusiasm in the seventeenth and early eighteenth centuries in England is briefly told; and this is followed by a résumé of theological and other controversies concerning enthusiasm. Finally, in the light of this history the position of the Methodists and their opponents is set forth.

CHAPTER I

ENTHUSIASM IN WESTERN CHRISTENDOM TO THE SEVENTEENTH CENTURY

IMMEDIATE inspiration was one of the two general classes of divination recognized in Cicero's well-known essay,[1] and the characteristic Greek word for it was "enthusiasm". Although the word itself came late into Greek literature, the idea was much earlier.[2] The theory of the sacred oracles, for example, was that of "a violent breaking forth of the divine spirit in a human body."[3]

The Thracian cult of Dionysos was based upon a similar belief. The devotee sought union with the godhead by drinking wine or by eating flesh, and the climax was reached in frenzies accompanied by prophetic utterances. Euripides' is the classic description:

[1] *De divinatione. M. Tulli Ciceronis Scripta quae Manserunt Omnia*, Recognovit A. F. W. Mueller, Part IV, vol. ii (Leipzig, 1878). An annotated text edited by Arthur Stanley Pease has been published in the *University of Illinois Studies in Language and Literature*, vol. vi, no. 2 (May, 1920), no. 13 (Aug., 1920) and vol. viii, no. 2 (May, 1923), no. 3 (Aug., 1923).

[2] On the word and its history *vide* article, "Enthusiasm" by Ludwig Radermacher in the *Encyclopedia of Religion and Ethics*. Edwyn Bevan's little book, *Sibyls and Seers* (London, 1928), gives a good brief survey of Greek theories of inspiration. There is also a short account in T. K. Oesterreich, *Possession* (New York, 1930), pp. 311-348.

[3] A. Bouché-Leclercq, *Histoire de la Divination dans l'Antiquité* (Paris, 1879-1882), vol. i, p. 372.

> A prophet is this god: the Bacchic frenzy
> And ecstasy are full-fraught with prophecy:
> For, in his fullness when he floods our frame,
> He makes his maddened votaries tell the future.[1]

Dionysos did not take a prominent place as a Greek prophet-god, but his cult contributed to the heightening of fervor in Greek religion; " offering no new ethical gospel," as Farnell says, yet Dionysos's religion did give " a more high-pitched mental life to man and woman, bondsman and free." [2] The present concern is only with the nature of Dionysos's enthusiasm. According to Rohde, the ἔνθεος was entirely in the god's power, speaking and acting at the will of the god.[3]

With Plato, inspiration becomes something other than seizure by a god. He speaks, in the *Phaedrus,* of four kinds of " madness ", prophecy, the inspiration by which one learns the method of deliverance from an ancient guilt, poetic afflatus, and love.[4] In the *Timaeus* he describes the state of the prophet: " No man in his wits attains prophetic truth and inspiration; but when he receives the inspired word, either his intelligence is enthralled in sleep, or he is demented by some distemper or possession." [5]

Poets are compared to Corybantian revellers and to Bacchic maidens:

---

[1] *The Bacchanals*, II, 298-301. Translation is from *Euripides with an English Translation* . . . (London and New York, 1912), Loeb Classical Library.

[2] L. R. Farnell, *The Cults of the Greek States,* vol. v (Oxford, 1909), p. 239. *Vide* also pp. 133 and 238. *Cf.* E. Rohde, *Psyche* (Freiburg i. B., 1898), bd. ii, pp. 19-20.

[3] Rohde, *op. cit.,* bk. ii, p. 20, n. 1. But *cf.* Oesterreich, *op. cit.,* pp. 341-4.

[4] *Phaedrus*, 244-251 (The references are to Jowett's translation).

[5] *Timaeus*, 71; *vide* also *Meno*, 99.

For the poet is a light and winged and holy thing, and there is no invention to him until he has been inspired and is out of his senses, and the mind is no longer in him: when he has not attained to this state, he is powerless and is unable to utter his oracles.[1]

The trend of the Platonic theory is disclosed in his treatment of philosophical inspiration. The philosopher is taken for a madman as he becomes rapt in the divine, for the vulgar "do not see that he is inspired."[2] In reality, he finds the divine by recollection:

For a man must have intelligence of universals, and be able to proceed from the many particulars of sense to one conception of reason; this is the recollection of those things which our soul once saw while following God, when, regardless of that which we now call being, she raised her head up towards the true being.[3]

Whether or not Plato intended his theory of reminiscence to be taken as a serious explanation of the philosopher's awareness of ideas, two things are plain: man has within him a spark of the divine, and he must turn away from particulars given by the senses if he would find the divine universals.

Without accepting any schematization of Plato's many-sided philosophy, one may see here the beginnings of certain tendencies by which primitive inspiration by enthusiasm was transformed into mystical ecstasy. Man is capable of inspiration because there is something divine in him; but the passivity of his bodily and mental powers under the inspiration of a god is not because of seizure by the god, but because of abstraction of the soul from the senses. The body is inimical to the soul; it drags down the higher

---

[1] *Ion*, 534.
[2] *Phaedrus*, 249.
[3] *Ibid.*

powers; only by turning from things can the soul perceive the divine.[1]

These two suggestions in Plato were developed by later thinkers. The Stoics emphasized the first, that man has in him something divine. They preached the immanence of the divine being: " In Him we live and move and have our being." On the other hand, Plotinus emphasized the distinction between body and soul; his inspiration is ecstasy, the union of the soul with the divine by rapture from bodily conditions.[2] In his own words:

We must hasten to depart hence, to detach ourselves as much as we can from the body to which we are unhappily bound, to endeavour to embrace God with all our being, and to leave no part of ourselves which is not in contact with him. Then we can see God and ourselves, as far as is permitted . . . we become divine, or rather we know ourselves to be divine.[3]

The present concern is not with mysticism defined as union of the soul with the Absolute whether in ecstasy or otherwise. Although a distinction between mysticism so defined and enthusiasm is somewhat arbitrary, it is necessary. This study is not concerned with a sense of presence or with unity with the Absolute attained by more or less philosophic mystics, but with the simpler, if vaguer idea of guidance, of impulses, information, commands coming directly from deity to the individual. Often, of course, this implied possession of the recipient by a god or a divine spirit

[1] *Phaedrus*, 246; *Republic*, bk. vii, 514-518.

[2] Radermacher, *Encyclopedia of Religion and Ethics*, art., " Enthusiasm."

[3] Ennead VI, ix, 9, *Plotini Enneades praemisso Porphyrii de vita Plotini deque ordine librorum eius libello* edidit Ricardus Volkmann (Lipsiae 1883-4), vol. ii, p. 522. The translation is quoted from William Ralph Inge, *The Philosophy of Plotinus*, second edition (London, 1923), vol. ii, pp. 139-140.

with the automatisms and other phenomena usually associated therewith. Consequently Neo-Platonism offers little, in theory, for the student of enthusiasm. Nor does the Latin world in general, for Roman divination was by other means than prophecy.[1]

Among the Semites one finds enthusiasm associated primarily with prophecy. Balaam, " falling but having his eyes open," is the classic example of Hebrew prophecy by trance.[2] Saul is said to have stripped off his clothes and to have prophesied before Samuel, before whom the king lay naked for a night and a day (I Samuel xix, 24). The same Hebrew word continued to be used to designate the " raving of the madman and the afflatus of the prophet."[3] Beginning with the eighth century B. C., the great prophets, while still feeling that the Spirit of the Lord came upon them, did not think of their own minds as in abeyance. The truth of their messages and the certainty of their inspiration rested upon their own consecration and upon their insight into the will of God.[4]

Nevertheless the older ideas persisted, as is witnessed by Philo, a Hellenized Jew, who enunciated a theory of inspiration which would have been acceptable alike to the ancient

---

[1] " Une âme humaine, possédée temporairement par l'esprit divin, dépouillée de son initiative et jusqu'à un certain point de sa personnalité, est un instrument trop delicat pour les dieux de l'Italie. Ils préfèrent, s'ils ne veulent que lancer dans le monde un mot mystérieux comme un oracle à la grecque, emprunter l'organ tout à tait passif des animaux. On voit souvent revenir dans la liste des prodiges que relatent les annales romaines la mention: ' Une vache a parlé '." Bouché-Leclercq, *op. cit.*, vol. iv, p. 132. Fowler agrees with this, *The Religious Experience of the Roman People* (London, 1911), p. 297 and note 12.

[2] Numbers xxiv, 4; George Adam Smith, *The Book of the Twelve Prophets,* (New York, n. d.), p. 15n.

[3] Ernest Findlay Scott, *The Spirit in the New Testament* (New York, pref. 1923), p. 23.

[4] *Vide* Scott, *op. cit.,* chap. viii.

Greek and to the more primitive Semite.[1] According to Philo all men possess the spirit in a limited degree, but full possession is only by divine gift. He himself many times had the experience of inspiration. Coming empty to his work he had had ideas "in an invisible manner showered" upon him and implanted in him from on high.[2] These personal experiences are reflected in Philo's theory of the inspiration of the Hebrew prophets, whom he thought of as the mechanical instruments of divine power.[3] In his well-known comment upon Genesis xv, 12, which he translates: "About the setting of the sun a trance fell upon him (Abraham)", Philo gives clear expression to his theory of inspiration:

As long therefore as our mind still shines around and hovers around, pouring as it were a noontide light into the whole soul, we, being masters of ourselves, are not possessed by any extraneous influence; but when it approaches its setting, then, as is natural, a trance which proceeds from inspiration, takes violent hold of us, and madness seizes us, for when the divine light shines the human light sets, and when the divine light sets this other rises and shines, and this very frequently happens to the race of prophets; for the mind that is in us is removed from its place at the arrival of the divine Spirit, but is again restored to its previous habitation when that Spirit departs, for it is contrary to holy law for what is mortal to dwell with what is immortal.[4]

[1] On Philo and his relation to Greek thought *vide* Hans Leisegang, *Der Heilige Geist. Das Wesen und Werden der Mystisch-Intuitiven Erkenntnis in der Philosophie und Religion der Griechen* (Leipzig-Berlin, 1919); Hans Lewy, *Sobria Ebrietas* (Giessen, 1929).

[2] *On the Migration of Abraham*, vii. The quotation is from the translation of C. D. Yonge, *The Works of Philo Judaeus* (London, 1854-5).

[3] James Drummond, *Philo Judaeus* (London, 1888), vol. i, p. 13; Henry Barclay Swete, *The Holy Spirit in the New Testament* (London, 1919), pp. 5-6.

[4] *On Who is the Heir of Divine Things*, liii (Yonge, *op. cit.*, vol. iv, p. 147).

Jesus did not have much to say that bears upon the question of enthusiasm, although he seems to have accepted the current theory of demoniacal possession. David is said to have spoken " by the Holy Ghost " (Mk. xii, 36) and " in the spirit "[1] (Mat. xxii, 43), but there is no elaboration of the idea of inspiration. On the other hand, Jesus does promise inspiration to his followers who are brought into judgment (Mk. xiii, 11).

In the Acts of the Apostles, one finds enthusiastic conduct recorded as a direct result of the operation of the Holy Spirit. The experience of Pentecost involved certain visual and auditory phenomena, the disciples acting almost as if drunken, and speaking " with tongues."[2] Similar phenomena attended the conversion of Cornelius and his company (Acts x, 44 *et seq.*) and the conversion of the followers of John the Baptist whom Paul met in Ephesus (Acts xix, 6). Three times in Acts the word " ecstasy " is used, each time in connection with prayer, to indicate the state in which an apostle receives divine revelation.[3] In the Book of Acts the general conception of inspiration seems to be that of the Old Testament, that the Spirit comes upon men intermittently giving them special powers.[4]

In the Pauline letters there is considerable reference to enthusiastic experiences. Paul himself had ecstatic visions, as in his conversion and in the experience referred to in II Corinthians xii. He also spoke " with tongues " and

---

[1] Mark xvi, 17 cannot be cited since it is generally regarded as a later addition to the text.

[2] A short treatment of this subject is in G. B. Cutten, *Speaking with Tongues* (New Haven, 1927).

[3] Acts x, 10; xi, 5; xxii, 17. *Vide* Henry Barclay Swete, *op. cit.*, p. 387; note K, " Rapture and Ecstasy," pp. 386-8.

[4] Scott, *op. cit.*, p. 83; F. J. Foakes Jackson and Kirsopp Lake [editors], *The Beginnings of Christianity* (London, 1920), part i, vol. ii, p. 194.

prayed and sang "with the spirit" (I Cor. xiv, 15, 18). The Pauline doctrine of the work of the Spirit is two-fold. He thought of the Spirit as producing Christian tempers and virtues (Gal. v, 22; I Cor. xiii, etc.). Salvation is a new creation, the formation of Christ in the believer (Gal. iv, 19) the putting on of Christ, as he calls it (Gal. iii, 27). The body is the temple of the Holy Spirit (I Cor. vi, 19). The indwelling of the Spirit or of Christ, for Paul speaks now of one, now of the other, is accompanied by the fruits of the Spirit, which are love, joy, peace (Gal. v, 22). But Paul also speaks of a spasmodic work of the Spirit to which he ascribes certain "gifts". In two passages he gives somewhat detailed account of these gifts. In Romans xii, 6 *et seq.*, he mentions prophecy, ministry, teaching, exhortation, giving, ruling and showing mercy. In I Corinthians xii, there is a longer list of gifts, which includes healing, prophecy and "divers kind of tongues."

The character of these charismatic gifts has been often discussed, and only prophecy and "divers tongues" need be mentioned here.[1] According to Paul, the prophet edified the church (I Cor. xiv, 4), and his prophesying was a sign to the church (v, 22). According to the Book of Acts, the prophet sometimes makes an authoritative announcement, as where Barnabas and Saul were separated for special work (Acts xiii, 1 *et seq.*) and Agabus prophesied future events (Acts xi, 28; xxi, 10 *et seq.*). The gift of prophecy was closely connected with the gift of discerning spirits, an indication that already there was need to distinguish between true and false prophets.

Among the most puzzling of charismata is the "gift of tongues." The fourteenth chapter of I Corinthians is given over to a discussion of this phenomenon, which seems to

[1] *Vide* Paul W. Schmiedel, art., "Spiritual Gifts" in *Encyclopaedia Biblica*, cols. 4769-70.

have been the cause both of confusion and of jealousy in the early church, since many coveted this spectacular gift. The Book of Acts speaks of the tongues at Pentecost as of different languages or dialects, but " tongues " in the Corinthian church refers to unintelligible speech.[1]

The confusion and jealousy arising, particularly in the Corinthian church, moved Paul to discriminate between the gifts and to lay down certain principles for the regulation of their exercise. A doctrinal test is imposed in I Corinthians xii, 3; no one can say, " Jesus is anathema," if he is speaking " in the Spirit of God "; and no one can say " Jesus is the Lord, but in the Holy Spirit." Paul values speaking with tongues less than prophecy and all such gifts less than love. This valuation is based on utility, for gifts are given for use. The Thessalonians are warned not to despise prophesyings nor to quench the Spirit, but also to prove all things. The spirit of the prophet is subject to the prophet; and he can regulate his conduct in the interests of order and peace (I Cor. xiv, 32-33).

In Paul's writings, then, one finds enthusiastic revelation and phenomena treated as genuine but as of lower value than the infused virtues of the Christian, and as in constant need of control. This control is by the church, which discerns spirits by doctrinal test, and also by individuals who have the special gift of discernment. Furthermore, enthusiasm is controlled by the enthusiast himself, who subjects his prophetic spirit to his will.

For some time after the Apostolic Age the charismatic gifts were said to be continuing. Justin Martyr asserts that miraculous powers existed in the church, and enumer-

[1] *Vide* Thomas M. Lindsay, *The Church and the Ministry in the Early Centuries* (London, n.d. Preface to second edition dated 1903), p. 47 n. 1, who follows Weiszäcker in considering speaking with tongues as ejaculatory prayer.

ates prophecy, healing and exorcism. Irenaeus adds gifts of tongues and raising the dead. Tertullian speaks of exorcism and tells of at least one prophetess.[1] Evidence for the existence of prophets in the years succeeding the apostles appears also in the *Didache* and in the *Shepherd of Hermas*. The Didache gives instructions as to the discernment of the spirit of the prophets. A prophet is not to be tried or judged, if he speaks in the Spirit; but if he orders a meal in the Spirit and eats of it, he is false; if he calls for money in the Spirit or if he practices not what he preaches, he is false.[2] *The Shepherd of Hermas* is itself an example of enthusiastic literature, of a prophetic message delivered in the form of visions. Its tests of a prophet are partly ethical: " Test, then, from his life and deeds the man who says he is inspired." [3] Another test repudiates such a conception as that of I Sam. ix, 9. The prophet is not consulted as a soothsayer " nor does he speak by himself (for the Holy Spirit does not speak when a man wishes to speak), but he speaks at that time when God wishes him to speak." [4]

This conception of prophecy, which is more in line with the Judaism of Philo than with Paul, is given expression again by the author of the *Hortatory Address to the Greeks*, once attributed to Justin, who says of the canonical prophets that they presented themselves " pure to the energy of the Divine Spirit, in order that the divine plectrum itself, descending from heaven and using righteous men as an instrument like a harp or lyre, might reveal to us the knowledge

[1] For this evidence, *vide* B. B. Warfield, *Counterfeit Miracles* (New York, 1918), pp. 11-15.

[2] *Didache,* chap. xi.

[3] Mandate xi, 16.

[4] Mandate xi, 9. Translations from the *Shepherd of Hermas* are from Kirsopp Lake, *The Apostolic Fathers with an English Translation,* 2 vols. (London and New York, 1913), The Loeb Classical Library.

of things divine and heavenly." [1] This was also the theory of Montanism.

The conservative, rigoristic, enthusiastic movement which arose in the Phrygian church about the middle of the second century was partly a protest against the growing organization of the church and against the spirit of accommodation with pagan society; but its most distinguishing characteristic was prophetism. Eusebius declares that Montanus " in a sort of frenzy and ecstasy " prophesied in " a manner contrary to the constant custom of the Church handed down by tradition from the beginning." [2] Harnack argues that Montanism cannot be put in the same category with early Christian prophecy, but that there was in Montanism a claim to a peculiar relation to the Spirit.[3] The claim was made that Montanus and some of his immediate followers were peculiarly inspired, that Montanus was the Paraclete promised in the Gospel of John, and that he had come to prepare the way for the millennial kingdom spoken of in the Apocalypse; but the chief objection to the Montanists was to the manner rather than to the matter of their prophecy.[4] The Montanists not only received their message in ecstasy, but they also spoke in ecstasy and in an ecstasy which was deliberately induced. The opponents of Montanism contended

[1] *Hortatory Address*, chap. viii. The translation is by Marcus Dods in *The Ante-Nicene Fathers,* American edition, vol. i (New York, c. 1885).

[2] Eusebius, *Church History,* bk. v, chap. xiv, 7, McGiffert's translation in *Nicene and Post-Nicene Fathers,* second series (New York, 1890).

[3] Adolf Harnack, *History of Dogma,* English Translation (Boston, 1905), vol. ii, p. 99. But *vide* Lindsay, *op. cit.,* p. 239 *et seq.* Phrygia was the home of religious excesses; as Franz Cumont puts it, " Violent ecstasies was always an endemic disease in Phrygia." (*The Oriental Religions in Roman Paganism.* Chicago, 1911, p. 50.)

[4] *Vide* note by A. C. McGiffert to Eusebius, *op. cit.,* bk. v, chap. 16, 7, in *Nicene and Post-Nicene Fathers,* vol. i, p. 231.

that true prophets are of sound mind, even during their ecstasy.[1]

As a result of the Montanist controversy, prophetism was discredited in the church. Montanist excesses compelled the church to define her theory of prophecy,[2] and the organization of the church against which the Montanists rebelled was hardened in reaction from their excesses; so that Irenaeus, at the close of the second century, could make the test of a prophet's genuineness his willingness to obey the elders in the church.[3]

With a three-fold emphasis upon the canon, correct doctrine and the authority of the church, came a growing conviction that the extraordinary gifts of the Spirit as they had been known in the Apostolic Age had ceased.[4] Christians were agreed on the existence of demoniacs among the pagans,[5] but they did not, as a rule, expect the unusual enthusiastic gifts of pre-Montanist Christianity. The older view that the Spirit might be expected to come in a special manner upon any Christian was giving way to a belief that the extraordinary gifts of the Spirit were restricted within the ecclesiastical organization.

Nevertheless, the church by no means denied the possibility of immediate divine inspiration. If demons could

[1] Hugh Jackson Lawlor, art. "Montanism," *Encyclopedia of Religion and Ethics*. On inspiration and ecstasy, *vide* E. Mangenot, art. "Inspiration de L'Écriture" in *Dictionnaire de Théologie Catholique*. No further comments need be made here on a movement so well known as Montanism. On the whole movement *vide* P. Champagne de Labriolle, *Les sources de l'histoire du montanisme* (Fribourg, 1913); *La crise montaniste* (Paris, 1913); Wilhelm Schepelern, *Der Montanismus und die Phrygischen Kulte* (Tübingen, 1929).

[2] Lindsay, *op. cit.*, p. 239 *et seq.*

[3] *Ibid.*, p. 213.

[4] Harnack, *op. cit.*, vol. ii, pp. 107-8.

[5] T. Ortolan, art. "Démoniaques" in *Dictionnaire de Théologie Catholique*.

move men to foretell the future, obviously God could do the same.[1] Indeed Augustine, in condemning murderers, excepts those who, like Samson, have secret instructions of the Spirit;[2] and in the case of a woman who drowned herself to protect her honor, he somewhat grudgingly allows that she, like Samson, might have had secret divine authority.[3]

It is no part of the present purpose to write a history of immediate inspiration in Western Christendom, but only to insist upon the continuance through the Middle Ages of belief in its possibility.[4] Much that was called prophecy was, of course, only interpretation of Scripture, as seems to have been true with Joachim of Fiore.[5] When a Franciscan, one John of Rupescissa, was imprisoned at Avignon in 1356, he was called upon by the Archbishop of Toulouse to predict the duration of the French wars. In answer he is said to have replied: ". . . . ea quae dico, non dico de capite meo, nec sum Propheta, sed tantum per intelligentias Prophetarum."[6] But claims to special commissions or to

---

[1] For Augustine's explanation of demoniac inspiration, *vide De divinatione daemonum,* iii (*Corpus Scriptorum Ecclesiasticorum Latinorum,* vol. xxxxi, sect. v, pars. iii, pp. 603-4).

[2] *De Civitate Dei,* lib. i, cap. xxi.

[3] *Ibid.,* lib. i, cap. xxvi.

[4] For a sketch of the history of Prophecy in the Middle Ages, *vide* Döllinger, " Der Weissagungsglaube und das Prophetentum in der christlichen Zeit," in his *Kleinere Schriften* (Stuttgart, 1890), pp. 451-557. This was translated into English in *Fables respecting the Pope in the Middle Ages, together with Dr. Döllinger's essay on the Prophetic Spirit,* etc. (New York, 1872). As an example of prophecy *cf.* St. Hildegard (1098-1179) in Henry Osborn Taylor, *The Medieval Mind* (London, 1914), vol. i, pp. 462-475; Lynn Thorndike, *Magic and Experimental Science in the First Thirteen Centuries of our Era* (New York, 1923), chap. xi, vol. ii, pp. 124-154.

[5] Döllinger, *op. cit.,* pp. 514-5.

[6] D'Argentré, *Collectio judiciorum de novis erroribus* . . . . *Lutetiae*

infallible information from the Almighty were common enough, as is evidenced by polemical writings against heretics. The preaching of the Waldenses, for example, was condemned because the direct mission from God which they claimed was unsubstantiated either by good works or by miracles.[1] The chroniclers furnish plentiful instances of enthusiasm which was judged heretical by the orthodox. As examples may be cited the case of Thomas of Apuleia, who was arrested in Paris in 1388 and claimed to have a mission from the Holy Spirit. He was adjudged insane and his sentence commuted to life imprisonment.[2] A heresiarch was arrested at Speyer in 1356 and accused of holding, among other errors, that an unlearned layman, without knowledge of the Scriptures but illuminated by divine afflatus such as he himself claimed, was a better teacher than a priest.[3]

In spite of these condemnations, however, the possibility of inspiration was carefully maintained. One of the errors attributed to Averroes was a belief that prophecy is by means of the natural faculties,[4] and in 1276 Bishop Stephen of Paris listed as heretical the statement that raptures and visions are by natural means.[5] Indeed the Canon Law, in

Parisiorum .... MDCCXXVIII, vol. i, I, p. 375, cols. 1 and 2. Rupescissa's writings consisted of his *Visions*, a *Commentary on the Oracles of Cyril* and his *Vade mecum in tribulationes*. For a short account of Rupescissa and his political prophecies, *vide* Franz Kampers, "Über die Prophezeiungen des Johannes de Rupescissa," *Historisches Jahrbuch*, vol. xv (Munich, 1894), pp. 796-802.

[1] Alanus ab Insulis, *Contra Haereticos Liber Quatuor*, lib. ii, cap. i (Migne, PL., vol. 210, col. 378C).

[2] D'Argentré, *op. cit.*, I, II, p. 151.

[3] *Ibid.*, I, I, p. 377.

[4] Eymerich, *Directorium Inquisitorum* .... Rom. MDLXXVIII, pars. II, quaestio iiii (I), p. 176, col. 4.

[5] D'Argentré, *op. cit.*, I, I, p. 199.

guarding against false pretensions to divine mission, expressly recognized the possibility of a true claim.[1]

A definition of the Church's position was given by Thomas Aquinas in his discussion of grace. According to him grace is two-fold, First, there is the grace by which a man is sanctified, an inner grace which renders man holy and pleasing to God. This grace Thomas calls "ingratiating" grace or "sanctifying" grace, *gratia gratum faciens*. The other kind of grace is that which is given to man for the instruction of others and confers supernatural gifts. This he calls *gratia gratis data*.[2] The former is common to all members of the church, the latter restricted to certain individuals,[3] not all grace which is given to man by God is called grace gratuitously given, but only that which exceeds the natural powers. Wisdom and knowledge, for example, are not ascribed to *gratia gratis data* except when they are in such abundance that a man may instruct others and overcome adversaries.[4] The *gratia gratis data* is differentiated according as it manifests itself in knowledge

---

[1] *Corpus Juris Canonici*, Decret. Greg. IX, lib. 5, tit. 7 de haeret., c. 12, ap. Friedberg II, col. 786; Potthast, *Regesta Pontificum Romanorum inde ab anno Christi n. MCXCVIII ad a. MCCCIV* (Berlin, 1874-5), no. 780. In the glossa ordinaria which Eymerich gives, there is a warning against too readily believing a miracle. (*Directorium Inquisitorum*, pars. ii, p. 93, col. Ib, 1578 ed.)

[2] *Secundum hoc igitur duplex est gratia. Una quidem per quam ipse homo Deo conjungitur: quae vocatur gratia gratum faciens. Alia vero per quam unus homo cooperatur alteri ad hoc quod ad Deum reducatur. Hujusmodi autem donum vocatur gratia gratis data, quia supra facultatem naturae, et supra meritum personae, homini conceditur. Summa Theologica,* pars prima secundae, cxi, art. 1. Cf. Joseph Pohle, art. "Grace," *Catholic Encyclopedia.* Latin quotations from St. Thomas are from *Sancti Thomae Aquinatis Angelici Opera Omnia Iussu Impressaque Leonis XIII, P. M. Edita* . . . . (Rome, 1892).

[3] Thomas Aquinas, *Summa,* pars prima secundae, quaestio cxi, art. v.

[4] *Summa,* pars prima secundae, quaestio cxi, art. iv.

(*cognitio*), in speech (*locutio*), or in works (*operatio*).[1] The nine " gifts " mentioned by Paul (I Cor. xii) are ascribed to these aspects of grace gratuitously given as follows: *cognitio*, prophecy, faith, discerning of spirits; *locutio*, word of wisdom, word of knowledge, interpretation and tongues; *operatio*, healing and other miracles.[2]

The *gratia gratis data* is given for use in convincing others: *Unicuique autem datur manifestatio Spiritus ad utilitatem* (I Cor. xii, 7) is the Scripture often quoted.[3] Matters which are subject to reasonable demonstration are proven by argument, but things which are above reason (*supra rationem*) are confirmed by divine manifestations.[4] This confirmation may be by miraculous works or healings (*operatio virtutum*); or by manifestations of divine powers, such as that the sun stands still or the sea is divided; or by manifesting such things as are known only to God, as by prophecy or the discerning of spirits.[5]

St. Thomas is decided in his opinion that prophecy does not require any special natural disposition.[6] Even the proper root of goodness, charity, is not a necessity, since charity is of the will, while the prophetic gift affects only the intellect. Baalam was inspired as were also the Sibyls who announced the coming of Christ.[7] These special gifts are subordinated to the authority of Scripture and dogma; on this the Church's position is admirably summarized by Cajetan (1469-1534) in his commentary on Aquinas:

Human actions are of two kinds, one of which relates to

[1] *Summa*, secunda secundae, quaestio clxxi.

[2] *Vide* commentaria of Cardinal Cajetan, intro. to quaestio clxxi.

[3] *Summa*, prima secundae, quaestio cxi, art. i.

[4] *Ibid.*

[5] *Ibid.*

[6] *Summa*, secunda secundae, quaestio clxxii, art. iii.

[7] *Ibid.*, quaestio clxxii, art. vi.

public duties, and especially to ecclesiastical affairs, such as preaching, celebrating Mass, pronouncing judicial decisions and the like; with respect to these the question is settled in the canon law, where it is said that no credence is to be publicly given to him who says he has privately received a mission from God, unless he confirms it by a miracle or by a special testimony of Holy Scripture. The other class of human actions consists of those of private persons, and speaking of these, he distinguished between a prophet who enjoins or advises them, according to the universal laws of the Church, and a prophet who does the same without reference to those laws. In the first case every man may abound in his own sense whether or not to direct his actions according to the will of the prophet; in the second case the prophet is not to be listened to.[1]

One further illustration of the medieval attitude toward enthusiasm may be given from a work ascribed to a famous chancellor of the University of Paris, John Gerson (1363-1429). In his *De probatione spirituum*,[2] Gerson insisted that it is dangerous either to approve false revelations or to fail to approve the true ones. Knowledge of the Holy Scripture and reason alone are not sufficient to prove the spirits: one must know something of their workings. He suggests certain questions which should be asked. It should be inquired whether those receiving the vision are of discreet judgment, whether they are novices, rich or destitute, learned or ignorant. The nature and end of the vision must also be examined; and one must consider whether the vision will

[1] Commentaria on secunda secundae, quaestio clxxiv, art. vi. The translation is the free rendering in art. "Prophecy" by Arthur Devine in *Catholic Encyclopedia*.

[2] *Opera* (Antwerp, 1706), vi, pp. 38-43. The *De probatione spirituum* was included in the 1580 edition of the *Malleus maleficarum*. It is quoted in modern Roman Catholic treatises on revelations, as in the article, "Discernement des Esprits," *Dictionnaire de Théologie*, t. iv, cols. 1390-1391; and Poulain, *The Graces of Interior Prayer*, Eng. trans. (London and St. Louis, n. d., imprimatur, 1910), pp. xxii, 60.

do the person who receives it any good. How does the person claiming the vision talk in public or in secret? This question is especially necessary if the inspired is a woman.

In such a discussion Gerson shows both his own sincere belief in the possibility of immediate inspiration and his realization of the dangers involved. This represents fairly the view of the Church and of learned men of the period. That the Church did not change its attitude during early modern times is known to all readers of the work which still regulates the process of beatification and canonization, the *De Servorum Dei Beatificatione et Beatorum Canonizatione* of Benedict XIV (1675-1758).[1] Benedict summed up the conclusions of previous writers, presenting them as the consensus of the Church. Prophecy is a *gratia gratis data,* and no natural disposition is requisite, not even charity; for at times the wicked have had the gift.[2] For this reason proof of a gift of prophecy is not sufficient for canonization; the saint must have had undoubted "heroic virtue." The belief of the ancients that fools, idiots and melancholy persons are more susceptible to inspiration is to be explained as referring to natural divination and not to true prophecy.[3] While ecstasy often accompanies revelation, it is not essential.[4] It is necessary that the prophet should know not only what is revealed to him but also that it is of God.[5] Moreover, a vision is not in itself enough to constitute a revelation to an individual, for the recipient must understand what he sees before he can be said to have had a private revelation.[6]

It would not be fair to say that the Roman Catholic church believes to-day that ecstatic prophecy or any other kind is necessarily or even probably authentic, but the

[1] Bologna (1734-8).
[2] Lib. iii, cap. xlvii.
[3] *Ibid.*, cap. xlvi, 4.
[4] *Ibid.*, cap. xlix, 14.
[5] *Ibid.*, xlv, 11.
[6] *Ibid.*, cap. ult.

Church does continue to hold to the reality of prophecy after the Apostolic Age. The canonization of Joan of Arc in 1920 involved a favorable judgment upon the divine origin of her visions; and only a French academician, embarrassed to steer between his patriotism and an offence to anti-clerical officialdom, would say, as Gabriel Hanotaux said, that at the ceremony of canonization, although the ecclesiastical advocate of Joan mentioned miracles, " la pensée universelle et sa propre pensée sont ailleurs; Jeanne d'Arc, c'est l'héroïne, la Sainte de la Patrie." [1]

The Protestant Reformation ushered in a lively discussion of enthusiasm incited by the activities of various radicals whom their opponents lumped together as "Anabaptists." [2] The leaders of the Protestant Revolt were emphatic in their opposition when the import of appeals to immediate revelation was made clear to them. Luther was

[1] Gabriel Hanotaux, "La Canonisation de Jeanne D'Arc," in *Revue des Deux Mondes,* vol. 58 (15 Aug., 1920), pp. 673-694. The present doctrine of the Roman Catholic Church on private revelation is admirably summarized in the *Dictionnaire apologétique de la foi catholique,* art. " Révélation divine " (1927) : Révélations privées.—1. L'Eglise catholique les tient 1° pour *possibles,* puisqu'elle ne les écarte point *a priori* quand il y a lieu d'en soumettre à son jugement; 2° pour *reelles* en certains cas, puisqu'elle en a autorisé, approuvé même plusieurs, soit par des sentences permissives ou laudatives, soit par la canonisation de saints personnages auxquels elles avaient été faites, soit par l'approbation ou l'établissement de fêtes liturgiques basées sur elles ; 3° pour relativement *rares,* puisqu'elle les examine toujours, sinon avec une méfiance *positive,* du moins avec une extrême circonspection; 4° pour *nécessairement subordonnées* à la révélation publique, et même pour justiciables de la théologie, qui est toujours appelée à les juger à la lumière de la foi catholique ; 5° pour *étrangères* au dépôt de la révélation générale et universellement obligatoire, puisqu'elle ne considère jamais comme hérétiques ceux qui refusent de les admettre, encore quils puissent quelquefois, être, en cela, imprudents et témeraires.

[2] On certain mystics of the sixteenth century, *vide* R. M. Jones, *Studies in Mystical Religion* (London, 1909). The standard histories of the Reformation discuss the Anabaptists and their relation to the leaders of the Protestant Revolt.

first confronted with enthusiastic pretensions by some prophets who hailed from a little town, Zwickau, in Saxony, which was the center of the weaving trade. Three men, one of whom had been a pupil of Melanchthon, came to Wittenberg and won over Luther's helper, Carlstadt, to their views while Luther was confined in the castle of the Wartburg (1521-1522). These prophets claimed to have the inspiration of the Spirit, and they pleaded the Spirit's authority for their radical religious and social doctrines.[1] Melanchthon was somewhat inclined to favor the prophets and desired that Luther might meet them. Luther hurried home to Wittenberg and did meet them; but the argument, as might have been expected, had no results except to confirm each in his own opinion. The prophets attempted to silence Luther by appealing to their authority, crying, " The Spirit, the Spirit"; and Luther answered, characteristically enough, " I slap your spirit on the snout." [2] Luther succeeded in quieting Wittenberg, but the controversy left permanent traces in Luther's formulation of his own doctrine.

The Reformer's main polemic against the prophets is contained in his tract, *Widder de hymelischen propheten von den bildern und Sacrament* (Wittenberg, 1524).[3] Against the prophets Luther advanced the usual demand for a miracle; but he also insisted upon the depth of the prophet's religious experience as a sign of genuineness. In reply to Melanchthon's request that he meet the enthusiast, Luther wrote from the Wartburg on January 13, 1522:

[1] Preserved Smith, *The Life and Letters of Martin Luther* (Boston, 1911), chap. xii.

[2] D'Aubigné, *History of the Great Reformation of the Sixteenth Century in Germany, Switzerland, etc.* First American edition (New York, 1841-2), vol. iii, p. 184. *Cf.* Julius Köstlin, *Martin Luther* . . . 5th edition (Berlin, 1903), vol. i, pp. 510, 677.

[3] The British Museum copy was consulted. The tract (parts I and II) is in Weimar ed. of Luther's Works, Band 18 (1908), pp. 37-214.

In the first place, those who bear witness of themselves are not to be believed, but spirits must be proved. . . . For God never sent any one who was not either called by men or attested by miracles, not even His own son . . . Do not receive them if they assert that they come by mere revelation . . .

Pray search their innermost spirit and see whether they have experienced those spiritual straightenings, that divine birth, death and infernal torture: If you find their experiences have been smooth, bland, devout (as they say) and ceremonious, do not approve them, though they claim to have been snatched up to the third heaven . . . Divine Majesty does not speak directly; rather no man shall see Him and live. Nature bears no small stars and no insignificant words of God. . . . Try not to see even Jesus in glory until you have seen him crucified.[1]

Luther's opposition to the doctrine of immediate revelation was founded in his fundamental religious convictions. His doctrine of the priesthood of all believers made him insistent against a teaching that laid undue emphasis upon extraordinary gifts of special men. "Therefore I say I will hold by His common revelation to all men in the word and works of Christ."[2] He declares that he does not desire for himself that God should speak with him from the sky, or appear to him; but that he shall have the gift of baptism and brethren who may have the grace and the gift of the Spirit to exhort and to warn and to teach.[3] Luther insists upon Christ's historic life and work: those who desire to seek him "in some private way" betray him afresh; he must be sought "as He was and walked on earth."[4]

The enthusiasts' claim contradicted Luther's fundamental

[1] Quoted by Preserved Smith, *op. cit.*, p. 139.

[2] Quoted by Herrmann, *The Communion of the Christian with God*, English Translation (Oxford, 1895), p. 145.

[3] *Ibid.*, p. 145, n.

[4] *Ibid.*, p. 146.

doctrine of the Word and of the church. According to Luther, God deals with us in two ways: outwardly, by the words of the Gospel and the sacraments; inwardly, by the Holy Ghost and faith, together with other gifts.[1] The outward things must precede and the inward come later and by means of the outward. The fanatics reversed this order. The Schmalkaldic Articles, which Luther drew up in 1536, state his position clearly:

> And in those things that relate to the spoken and external Word, it must be steadfastly held that God bestows upon no one His Spirit or His grace except through the Word and along with the Word, as external and previously spoken, that so we may defend ourselves against enthusiasts, i. e., spirits who boast that they have the Spirit prior to the Word and without the Word and accordingly judge, twist, and pervert Scripture or the spoken word according as they please. . . . Wherefore we must steadfastly adhere to this, that it is not God's will to transact with us except through the spoken word and sacraments, and that whatever boasts itself without the Word and sacraments as Spirit is the Devil himself.[2]

In accord with his doctrine of the church, Luther insists that a minister must have a regular call by the congregation. "He who will come out as a minister must show a regular call, or else a miracle; wherever there is no stand made upon the call there should be left in the end no more a church."[3]

John Calvin was involved in controversy with the Anabaptists in 1537, and this dispute caused him to formulate

---

[1] J. A. Dorner, *History of Protestant Theology*, English translation by Rev. George Robson, M. A. (Edinburgh, 1871), vol. i, p. 144 *et seq.*

[2] Quoted by Harnack, *History of Dogma*, vol. vii, p. 249. But on Luther's doctrine of the outward and inner Word, *vide*, Grisar, *Luther* (St. Louis, 1913-17), vol. iv, pp. 391-8.

[3] Quoted by Dorner, *op. cit.*, vol. i, p. 173.

more carefully his criteria of Christian truth in order that he might avoid the traditionalism of the Roman Catholics on the one hand and the subjectivism of the radical sectaries on the other. The influence of this controversy with the Anabaptists is reflected in the different editions of the *Institutes*.[1]

Calvin's doctrine of the testimony of the Holy Spirit (*testimonium Spiritus Sancti*) was liable to misuse by those who wished to exalt the authority of the Spirit above the authority of the Scriptures. Calvin himself made the Bible the supreme religious authority, but the truths of the Scripture are "efficaciously impressed on our hearts by the Spirit." There is a

kind of mutual connection between the certainty of this Word and his Spirit; so that our minds are filled with a solid reverence for the word, when by the light of the Spirit we are enabled therein to behold the Divine countenance; and, on the other hand, without the least fear of mistake, we gladly receive the Spirit, when we recognize him in his image, that is in the word.[2]

But Calvin goes further than this: the inspiration of the Bible is authenticated by the testimony of the Holy Spirit in the heart of the believer.[3] This assertion might be taken to mean that Calvin exalted the direct testimony of the Spirit to the consciousness of the believer above even the written Word. To avoid such interpretation, Calvin inserted in later editions of the *Institutes* paragraphs that make his position clear:

[1] Karl Heim, *Das Gewissheitsproblem in der systematischen Theologie bis zu Schleiermacher* (Leipzig, 1911), p. 269 *et seq.* Also E. Doumergue, *Jean Calvin* (Lausanne, 1897-1927), vol. xiv, p. 4.

[2] John Calvin, *Institutes of the Christian Religion,* translated by John Allen, Memorial Edition (Philadelphia, 1909), bk. i, chap. ix, 3.

[3] *Ibid.,* bk. i, chap. vii, 4.

For there have lately arisen some unsteady men, who haughtily pretending to be taught by the Spirit, reject all reading themselves, and deride the simplicity of those who still attend to (what they style) the dead and killing letter. . . .

The office of the Spirit, then, which is promised to us, is not to feign new and unheard of revelations, or to coin a new system of doctrine, which would seduce us from the received doctrine of the Gospel, but to seal to our minds the same doctrine which the Gospel delivers.[1]

Both Luther and Calvin, therefore, opposed the claims of the enthusiasts with the supremacy of the Word. Luther insisted that the Spirit follows the Word and the sacraments; and Calvin held that the Spirit accompanies the Word testifying to its truth and enforcing it upon the heart of the believer. To both, the claim to immediate inspiration was rejected, not on any theory of inherent impossibility, but because of incompatibility with their doctrines of faith and of the church. Against Rome they had pleaded for the direct operation of the Spirit in the individual, but against the enthusiasts they limited that operation to the sanctifying graces and to authentication of the gospel in the Scriptures.

As a final illustration of the ideas prevailing in evangelical circles may be cited Caspar Peucer's *Commentarius de Praecipuis Divinationum Generibus* (Wittenberg, 1553). Peucer (1525-1602) was the son-in-law and counsellor of Melanchthon and was professor of mathematics and later of medicine in Wittenberg. Peucer recognizes a spiritual divination wherein one is given information by the unquestioned and immediate testimony of God. There is also a physical divination which consists in reasoning from cause to effect, and this is in principle a legitimate means of foretelling the future. He gives a medical description of melan-

---

[1] Calvin, *op. cit.*, bk. i, chap. ix, 1.

choly and ecstasy, but prefers to explain ecstatic visions by intervention of the devil.

From these illustrations of the history of the idea until the seventeenth century, it is evident that enthusiasm came into Christianity from both Greek and Hebrew sources. Through the medium of the early church the notion of immediate inspiration passed into medieval Catholicism, and the Catholic Church continued to believe in its possibility under certain conditions; but for various reasons the theologians of the Reformation on the whole denied the continuance of the extraordinary gifts of the spirit. The post-Reformation theologians restricted these to the Apostolic Age, but this view gave way to another which granted that the gifts remained in the Church for two or three centuries before ceasing altogether.[1] " Enthusiasm " became, therefore, for orthodox Protestants "a false claim to inspiration."

[1] *Vide* Warfield, *Counterfeit Miracles,* p. 6 *et seq.*

CHAPTER II

English Enthusiasm from the Times of the Westminster Assembly to those of the Methodist Movement

THE present study is concerned with enthusiasm in England during the century which lies between the Westminster Assembly and the beginning of Methodism. Controversy over the question never ceased. Although the Edwardian and Elizabethan articles were influenced by continental reformers, especially by Melanchton and the Augsburg Confession, yet there are many signs of the controversy on English soil. Of the Forty-two Articles of religion promulgated in the Church of England in 1553, the fifth, on "Sufficiency of Scripture," was probably written with the desire to discourage pretensions to immediate inspiration.[1] Writing in 1699, Bishop Burnet said that Article Seven of the Thirty-Nine Articles (1563), "Of the Old Testament," was framed with " an extravagant sort of enthusiasts " in mind. These enthusiasts were, according to Burnet, antinomians who obeyed not the outward law but " a new inward

[1] Charles Hardwick, *A History of the Articles of Religion* (Philadelphia, 1860), p. 101. In the *Reformatio Legum Ecclesiasticarum* .... (London, 1571), a redraft of Canon Law made by Cranmer and a commission, chapter 3, "De Haeresibus," refers to those who reject the authority of the Holy Scriptures: ". . . quarum praesens pestis perniciem religionis nostrorum temporum adhuc incubat. In quo genere teterrimi illi sunt (itaque a nobis primum nominabuntur), qui sacras Scripturas ad infirmorum tantum hominum debilitatem ablegant & detrudunt, sibi sic ipsi interim praefidentes, ut eorum spiritum iactant, a quo sibi omnia suppeditari aiunt quaecunque docent & faciunt" (p. 5).

nature."[1] In the next century the Westminster Confession (1647) betrays Presbyterian concern for the Scriptures as against inward voices. Article X reads:

> The Supreme Judge, by which all controversies of religion are to be determined, and all decrees of councils, opinions of ancient writers, doctrines of men, and private spirits, are to be examined, and in whose sentence we are to rest, can be no other but the Holy Spirit speaking in the Scripture.[2]

A survey of the confused religious scene in England of the latter seventeenth and early eighteenth centuries will make clear the persistence of the enthusiasm which had vexed the makers of the orthodox creeds.

The English Baptists were early divided into two camps, the Arminian and the Calvinistic. The Arminian, or General Baptists, arose in the Netherlands among a group of Independents who had fled from persecution in England and who had come under Mennonite (or Anabaptist) influence. The Calvinistic, or Particular Baptists, arose in England and apparently apart from direct Mennonite influence.[3]

In 1644, a confession of faith was put forth by seven Calvinistic Baptist churches in London.[4] This confession was of such a conservative character that even Doctor Featley, who had been a member of the Westminster Assembly and who had once held a public debate with the General Baptists at Southwark, said that, if the confession really represented

---

[1] Gilbert Burnet, *An Exposition of the Thirty-Nine Articles of the Church of England*. Revised and corrected .... by the Rev. James R. Page, A. M. (New York, 1842), p. 123.

[2] Philip Schaff, *The Creeds of Christendom* (New York, 1877-81), vol. iii, pp. 605-6.

[3] *Vide* Albert Henry Newman, art. "Baptists," *Encyclopaedia Britannica* and W. J. McGlothlin, *Baptist Confessions of Faith* (Philadelphia, c. 1911), pp. 50 and 168-169.

[4] This confession is reprinted in McGlothlin, *op. cit.*, pp. 171-189.

the position of the Baptists, then the English Baptists were only in part Anabaptist and had not "taken any lesson in the upper formes;"[1] but he thought that the confession was only "a little Ratsbane covered with a great quantity of sugar."[2] According to the confession, the authority of the Christian is the written word of God "contained in the Canonical Scriptures.[3] Pagitt attacked the 41st article for the statement "that such to whom God hath given gifts may preach. . . ." If the Anabaptistical calling be ordinary, said the heresiographer, "let them prove it by Scripture: if extraordinary, let them prove it by Miracles".[4]

The Arminian or General Baptists established their first church in England in 1612. Their position in regard to immediate inspiration may be seen from a confession of faith of one hundred articles, which was originally published in both Dutch and English, and which probably represents the final views of John Smyth, founder of the English Arminian Baptists. This confession was published in Amsterdam after Smyth's death in 1612, by his followers, and is a modification of a confession published during his lifetime. Article 53 is as follows:

That although ther be diverse gifts of the spirit, yet ther is but one spirit, which distributeth to every one as he will 2 Cor.

---

[1] Daniel Featley, *The Dippers dipt, or the Anabaptists Duck'd and Plung'd over Head and Eares* . . . (London, 1645), p. 220. The preface of the first edition is dated Jan. 10, 1644; the British Museum copy has a MS date, Feb. 7, 1644. Six editions were printed in six years, according to Joseph Ivimey, *A History of the English Baptists* (London, 1811), vol. i, p. 166. For an account of Featley's controversy with the Baptists, *vide* Ivimey, vol. i, pp. 164-167.

[2] Featley, *op. cit.*, p. 220. The phrase struck the fancy of Ephraim Pagitt, who used it in his *Heresiography: or, A description of the Hereticks and Sectaries of these latter Times* . . . (London, 1645), p. 42.

[3] McGlothlin, *op. cit.*, p. 176.

[4] Pagitt, *op. cit.*, p. 43.

12. 4, 11 : Eph. 4. 4 that the outward gifts of the spirit which the holy ghost powreth forth upon the day of pentecost upon the disciples, in tongues and prophecy, and giftes, and healing, and miracles, which is called the baptism of the holy ghost and fire Acts 1. 5 were onlie a figure of and an hand leading to better things, even the most proper gifts of the spirit of sanctification, which is the new creature, which is the one baptism Eph. 4. 4 compared with Acts 2. 33, 38 and with Lucke 10. 17, 20.[1]

But the direction in which the Arminian Baptists could look, in spite of this orthodox statement, became evident from other articles of this confession:

60. That such as have not attained the new creature, have need of the scriptures, creatures and ordinances of the church, to instruct them, to comfort them, to stir them upp the better to performe the condicion of repentance to the remission of sins.

61. That the new creature which is begotten of God, needeth not the outwoard scriptures creatures or ordinances of the church, to support or help them, seeing he hath three witnesses in himself, the father, the word, and the holie ghost: which are better than all scriptures, or creatures whatsoever.[2]

These latter articles are safeguarded by the statement that the regenerate will use the outward things of the church for the sake of others, so that outward things are always necessary. Moreover, while the new creature is above the law and scripture, he can yet do nothing contrary to them.[3]

In a petition presented to James I in 1620 and thought to have been written by members of the first Arminian Baptist Church, the rule of faith is declared to be the Holy Ghost " contained in the sacred scriptures." The Spirit of God to

---

[1] John Smyth, *Works* (Cambridge, 1915), vol. ii, p. 742. This confession is reprinted from the only copy known to be in existence, which was found in York Minster Library.

[2] Smyth, *op. cit.*, vol. ii, pp. 743-4. Scripture references are omitted.

[3] *Ibid.*, Articles 62 and 63.

interpret the scriptures is given all "that fear and obey God." Commonly the Spirit is given to "the simple, poor, despised, etc.;" the learned do not usually learn the secrets of God.[1]

In the *Last Book of John Smyth*, there is a statement which further illustrates Baptist doctrine. Smyth says:

... although it be lawfull to pray preach, and sing out of a booke for all penitent persons, yet a man regenerate is above all bookes and scriptures whatsoever, seeing he hath the spirit of God within him which teacheth him the true meaning of the scriptures, without which spirit the scriptures are but a dead letter, which is perverted and misconstrued, as we see at this day, to contrary ends and sences: and that to bind a regenerate man to a booke in prayinge, preachinge, or singeinge, is to sett the Holy Ghost to school in the one as well as the other.[2]

This is in line with opposition to the Prayer Book by certain groups within the Church of England; but that some Baptists went to swell the ranks of the enthusiastic sects whose characteristics will be noticed in later paragraphs is evident from the concern of the orthodox groups to deny any connection between Baptist principles and such falling away. The Particular Baptists published an address entitled "Heart-bleedings for Professors' Abominations," which they appended to later editions of the 1644 Confession, and which contained a plea against the views of the Quakers and Ranters and denied that Baptist views led to such positions as the radical sectaries held.[3] The General Baptists, in 1678,

---

[1] *A most humble supplication of many of the King's Majesty's loyal subjects* ... (1620), reprinted in *Hanserd Knollys Society Publications*, vol. i, pp. 182-231. This, of course, is similar to Luther's position and perhaps not more dangerous than Calvin's *testimonium spiritus sancti*.

[2] *Works*, vol. ii, p. 755. *Cf.* "Certayne demaundes from the auncyent brethren of the Separation" (vol. ii, pp. 324-5). Smyth does not seem to have meant any disparagement of the Bible.

[3] McGlothlin, *Baptist Confessions of Faith*, p. 199. The address is reprinted in *Hanserd Knollys Society Publications*, vol. x, pp. 239-310.

under pressure of the suspicion that fell upon the Baptists following the Fifth Monarchy uprisings, issued what is called their "Orthodox Creed," which approached as nearly as was possible for Arminians to the position of the Calvinistic Baptists. In this confession, they explicitly rejected dependence upon immediate inspiration: "Neither ought we, since we have the scriptures delivered to us now, to depend upon, hearken to, or regard the pretended immediate inspirations, dreams, or prophetical predictions, by or from any person whatsoever, lest we be deluded by them."[1]

From a consideration of the orthodoxy of the Church of England, of the Presbyterians and of the main body of the Baptists one must turn to individuals and groups more justly accused of tenderness toward enthusiasm.

The mystical side of English religious life received fresh impetus during the disturbed years of the Rebellion and of the Commonwealth. One source of this mystical influx may have been the writings of Jacob Boehme (1575-1624), the German mystic, which were translated into English about 1648.[2] But whatever the sources, the disturbed conditions furnished fertile soil for mystical and enthusiastic ideas. There were first of all individuals who were distinctly mystics. Notable examples are William Dell (d. 1664), Master of Gonville and Caius College, Cambridge, and Henry More (1614-1687), the Cambridge Platonist. These mystics were not always thoroughgoing in their theology and sometimes held self-contradictory views of God and the world; but on the whole they represent the mystical instead of the

[1] McGlothlin, *op. cit.*, p. 152.

[2] On the whole field of seventeenth-century mysticism in England, *vide* Rufus M. Jones, *Studies in Mystical Religion* (London, 1909) and *Spiritual Reformers in the 16th and 17th Centuries* (London, 1914). For an attempt to trace the influence of Boehme in England, particularly in Milton, *vide* Margaret Lewis Bailey, *Milton and Jakob Boehme* (New York, 1914).

enthusiastic according to the distinction adopted for the purpose of this study.[1]

In addition to individual mystics, there arose in those unsettled days a number of sects which troubled the souls of the more orthodox Episcopalians, Presbyterians and Independents. These sects seemed to the orthodox to be proceeding against all authority in religion. Even the Leveller, John Lilburne,[2] who himself afterwards became a Quaker, was shocked by the multitude of different groups and opinions that sprang up.

> I had it from a Brother of mine in tribulation, and a fellow sufferer; who though he differs from me in opinion, yet I truly love him and shall never decline any christian office to do him good for soule and body; I meane M. John Lillburne, Lieutenant Colonel, who himself related it unto me, and that in the presence of others, that returning from the warres to London, he met forty new Sects, and many of them dangerous ones; and some so pernicious, that howsoever, as he said, he was in his judgment for toleration of all Religions; yet he profest, he could scarce keep his hands off them, and had no patience to hear theme so blasphemous they were in their opinions.[3]

Thomas Edwards (1599-1647), a Presbyterian controversialist who zealously gathered all the information to the dis-

---

[1] *Vide supra*, p. 16.

[2] John Lilburne (1614?-1657), political agitator and advocate of advanced social and political views. *Vide infra*, pp. 104-5.

[3] From John Bastwick's *The Second Part of that Book called Independency Not God's Ordinance: or The Post-script* (London, 1645), p. 37. Cf. Hetherington, *History of the Westminster Assembly of Divines*, fourth edition (Edinburgh, 1878), p. 143, n. For a survey of the sectaries, vide David Masson, *The Life of John Milton* (London, 1876), vol. iii, pp. 136-159. This account is a fair summary of contemporary discussions, but much fuller information is contained in Robert Barclay, *The Inner Life of the Religious Societies of the Commonwealth* (London, 1876). *Vide supra*, for reference to works of Rufus M. Jones.

credit of the heretical sects that he could find and published it in the three parts of his *Gangraena* (London, 1645), catalogues " Errours, Heresies, Blasphemies " to the number of 176; but he says that all can be referred to sixteen sorts of sectaries:

1. Independents. 2. Brownists. 3. Chiliasts, or Millenaries. 4. Antinomians. 5. Anabaptists. 6. Manifestarians or Arminians. 7. Libertines. 8. Familists. 9. Enthusiasts. 10. Seekers and Waiters. 11. Perfectists. 12. Socinians. 13. Arians. 14. Antitrinitarians. 15. Antiscripturists. 16. Scepticks and Questionists, who question everything in matters of Religion; namely all the Articles of Faith, and first Principles of Christian Religion, holding nothing positively nor certainly, saving the doctrine of pretended liberty of conscience for all, and liberty of Prophesying.[1]

That the sectaries were really disturbing the peace of the churches is evident from a petition of the ministers of London to the House of Commons, September 18, 1644, setting forth that:

Through many erroneous opinions, ruinating Schismes and damnable heresies (unhappily fomented in City and Countrey) the Orthodox Ministry is neglected; the people seduced; Congregations torne asunder; families distracted; rights and duties of relations, Nationall, Civill and Spirituall, scandalously violated; the power of godliness decayed; Parliamentary Authority undermined, fearfull confusion introduced; imminent destruction threatened, and in part inflicted upon us lately in the West.[2]

Undoubtedly there was much hysteria among the orthodox, but their state of mind is evident enough. Throughout the 1640's they continued to publish such tracts as these: *A*

[1] *Gangraena,* part i, p. 15.
[2] *The humble Petition of the Ministers of the City of London* (London, 1644).

Discovery of 29 sects here in London, all of which except the first are most Divelish and Damnable . . . (London, 1641); *A Swarme of Sectaries, and Schismatiques; wherein is discovered the strange preaching (or prating) of such as are by their trades Coblers, Tinkers, Pedlers, Weavers, Sow-gelders, and Chymney Sweepers* . . . (London, 1641. This was by John Taylor, the water-poet); *Truths Victory against Heresie; All sorts comprehended under these ten mentioned* . . . (London, 1645); *Vindiciae Veritatis or an Unanimous Attestation to Gods blessed Truth Revealed in his Word: Together with a serious Protestation against those Church-desolating and Soul-damning Errors, Heresies, and Blasphemies, which of late have come like a flood upon our County and Kingdome* . . . (London, 1648). It was a period which the orthodox were to look back upon as those " late unhappy times when Hell was broke loose." [1]

With outer restraints temporarily removed and the country in turmoil, there was a revival of claims to both prophecy and miracles. Men like Cromwell listened soberly to those who claimed special gifts. In the Council of the Army, grave argument as to how the Spirit of God could be discerned took the time of leaders assembled to look after the interests of the country.[2] On one such occasion, Cromwell declared that when one spoke as from God the rule should be: " Lett the rest judge!" [3] Public claims to the power to cleanse lepers, to heal defective sight and to make the lame to walk were made and sponsored by prominent persons.[4]

[1] Thomas Comber, *Christianity no Enthusiasm* (London, 1678), p. 88.

[2] Robert Barclay, *op. cit.,* p. 218. *Cf.* the prophecy of Elizabeth Poole before the General Council at Whitehall, December 29, 1648: *vide* Charles Harding Firth [ed.], *The Clarke Papers* (London, 1891-1894), vol. ii, p. 150.

[3] *The Clarke Papers,* vol. i, pp. 375-6.

[4] *Vide* Barclay, *op. cit.,* pp. 216 et seq.

The disturbed condition of religious men who longed for a satisfying faith, but who were religiously adrift, is typified in the groups and individuals called " Seekers " or " Waiters." These are described by Bastwick as follows:

Many of them have jangled so long about the Church, that at last they quite have lost it, & goe under the name of *Expectants* and *Seekers* & doe deny that there is any true Church or any true Ministers, or any Ordinances; some of them affirme that the Church is yet in the wildernesse, and they are seeking for it there: others say that the smoke is yet in the Temple, and they are groping for it there, where I leave them: praying God to open their eyes and give them repentance; that they may consider from whence they are fallen, and return again to the bosome of that Church, from which they have, to the great dishonour of God, and the scandalizing of the Gospel, made so fearfull a defection.[1]

With this description by an opponent may be compared the account of a Seeker, who agrees that all should search the Scriptures and practise prayer and alms:

Expressing their deep sence of the want of what they enjoy not, behaving themselves as persons having neither power or gift to go one before another, by way of Eminency or Authority; but as Sheep unfolded, and as Souldiers uncalled, waiting for a time of gathering, and restitution to the knowledge of what as yet they understood not: and the attainment of this is the end of their seeking; and to this they stirre up and provoke one another; and herein they desire to be found, hoping firmly to the end . . .[2]

---

[1] Bastwick, *op. cit.*, pp. 37-8. Pagitt liked this paragraph so well that he inserted it (with some mistakes) in his second edition of *Heresiography*, p. 141.

[2] *A Sober Word To a Serious People: Or, A Moderate Discourse Respecting as well the Seekers, (so called) As the Present Churches.* . . . (London, 1651), p. 3.

Among such groups bizarre doctrines found hearty welcome. Episcopal, Presbyterian or Independent, all were alike unsatisfactory; the " sheep unfolded " would follow any pleasant piper.

Prominent in all the lists compiled by heresiographers is the Family of Love, founded in the sixteenth century by Hendrick Niclas. Possibly never very numerous in England, the Familists were reduced to about three score in 1687, and these chiefly in the Isle of Ely, according to a petition presented to James II.[1] They seem, however, to have attracted some persons of quality.[2] The Familists disclaimed connection with the Puritans, the Brownists and the Anabaptists in a supplication presented to James I in 1606;[3] and their theological views were clearly mystical. Niclas exhorted his followers to despise gifts and to give their " understanding captive under the obedience of the love in the spirit. . . . For the love is the fulfilling of all this, and the divine being itself; and it is the true life and holy wisedome promised for to come, to a shining of Jerusalem round about."[4] Samuel Rutherford said that " the Familists make God in his nature and essence to dwell and worke in all creatures, especially the regenerate."[5] Pagitt gives their doctrine of Christ as follows: " Christ is not one man; but

[1] Evelyn's *Diary,* Entry of June 16, 1687.

[2] Etherington, *A Brief Discovery of the Blasphemous Doctrine of Familisme.* . . . (London, 1645), p. 10.

[3] Barclay, *Inner Life of the Religious Societies,* p. 27.

[4] *An Introduction to the Holy Understanding of the Glasse of Righteousness.* . . . (London, 1649), pp. 82-3. The British Museum has also *Introductio. An introduction to . . . . the glasse of Righteousness,* printed perhaps in 1575.

[5] Rutherford, *A Survey of the Spiritual Antichrist* (London, 1648), book i, p. 17. Rutherford (1600-1661) was a Scottish minister and one of the commissioners of the Church of Scotland to the Westminster Assembly, 1643.

an estate and condition in men common to so many as have received H. N. (Hendrick Niclas) his doctrine, etc."[1] Salvation was defined in a mystical sense: "All illuminated Elders are godded with God, or deified; and God Hominified, or become man."[2]

There seems to have been an ecstatic character to their actions. Richard Baxter (1615-1691), the well-known preacher and theologian, had an "old, godly friend" who lived near the Familists who were called Grundletonians (more properly Grindletonians, from the name of a village in Yorkshire). This friend of Baxter went once among the Familists, " and they breathed on him as to give him the Holy Ghost; and his family, for three days after, perceived him as a man of another spirit, as half in an ecstasy, and after that he came to himself, and came near them no more ".[3]

In regard to religious authority, the Familists seem to have been at one with all mystics in exalting the inner consciousness above outer regulation. Pagitt says the " Grindletonian Familists " held the Scriptures " but for Novices," and that " their spirit is not to be tryed by the Scripture, but the Scripture by their spirit."[4] He also asserts that the Familists held the writings of Hendrick Niclas to be of equal authority with the Scriptures.[5] Rutherford adds that they considered human industry and arts and sciences vain;[6] and Etherington reports that a Familist by the name of Randall

[1] Pagitt, *op. cit.*, p. 78.

[2] *Ibid.*, p. 79.

[3] Richard Baxter " Of the Sin Against the Holy Ghost," *Practical Works* (London, 1854), vol. ii, p. 344.

[4] Pagitt, *op. cit.*, p. 83.

[5] *Ibid.*, p. 79.

[6] Rutherford, *op. cit.*, bk. i, pp. 45, 79.

preached in London, in 1645, " that a man baptized with the Holy Ghost knew all things even as God knew all things." [1]

The most important of the sects appearing in this period and claiming authority for the deliverance of the individual's consciousness was the Friends. The Friends, or Quakers, began with the ministry of George Fox (1624-1691), the son of a Leicestershire weaver. After a spiritual pilgrimage similar to that of the Seekers, Fox found a satisfying experience and doctrine which he proclaimed for forty years throughout England and Scotland and abroad in Holland and America. Fox's first propagandist work was in 1647. This work was mainly among groups which had broken with the established church and had fellowship together, as the " shattered " Baptist church at Mansfield which developed into the earliest Quaker congregation.[2] By the end of 1660 the Quakers numbered between thirty and forty thousands out of a population of approximately five millions.[3] Owing to extensive emigrations to America, the figures for the Quakers at the end of the century are possibly not much larger.[4]

Fox claimed to have received his message by inspiration:

These things I did not see by the help of man, nor by the

---

[1] Etherington, *A Brief Discovery*, p. 2. On Randall *vide* Jones, *Spiritual Reformers*, pp. 253-263.

[2] William Charles Braithwaite, *The Beginnings of Quakerism* (London, 1912), pp. 12, 53, 130.

[3] *Ibid.*, p. 512.

[4] Braithwaite, *The Second Period of Quakerism* (London, 1919), pp. 457-60. The Quakers seem to have been regarded as more important than their numbers would indicate. As an evidence of their importance, Braithwaite points out (*Beginnings of Quakerism,* p. 305) that out of 98 writers against the Quakers recorded in Smith's *Bibliotheca Anti-Quakeriana,* 37 are to be found in the *Dictionary of National Biography.* The Society for the Promotion of Christian Knowledge and the Society for the Propagation of the Gospel both made special efforts for the conversion of Quakers (*Second Period of Quakerism,* pp. 492, 496).

letter, though they are written in the letter; but I saw them in the light of the Lord Jesus Christ, and by His immediate spirit and power, as did the holy men of God by whom the Holy Scriptures were written. Yet I had no slight esteem of the Holy Scriptures, they were very precious to me, for I was in that Spirit by which they were given forth: and what the Lord opened in me, I afterwards found was agreeable to them.[1]

He urged others to seek within for God, to turn to the inner light which he " infallibly knew would never deceive any." [2] Those who turn to the light within must turn from outward churches and ordinances, " from their churches, which men had made and gathered, to the Church in God, the general assembly written in heaven, which Christ is the head of. . . ." Men were called, in short, from

Jewish ceremonies, and from heathenish fables, and from men's inventions and windy doctrines, by which they blew the people about, this way and other way, from sect to sect; and from all their beggarly rudiments, with their schools and colleges for making ministers of Christ, who are indeed ministers of their own making but not of Christ's; and from all their images and crosses, and sprinkling of infants, with all their holy days (so called) and all their vain traditions, which they had gotten up since the apostles' days, which the Lord's power was against.[3]

This teaching is very similar to that of other of the early Dissenters; but the doctrine of the inner light preached among unstable listeners, led to extravagancies. In 1650 James Nayler,[4] a gifted preacher but apparently unsettled by

[1] *The Journal of George Fox, A Revised text prepared and edited by Norman Penney, F.S.A.* (London and Toronto, pref. 1924), p. 20.

[2] *Ibid.,* p. 21.

[3] *Ibid.,* pp. 21-22.

[4] On Nayler, *vide* Braithwaite, *The Beginnings of Quakerism,* chap. xi.

the adulation of his followers, rode into Bristol in a sort of triumphal entry, with a courier running bare-headed in front of him, another leading his horse, and women spreading their scarfs before him. For this Nayler was imprisoned and later sentenced to barbarous punishment for blasphemy. His real opinions seem to have been more mystical than enthusiastic. The following excerpts are from a contemporary account of his trial:

Q. Art thou the only son of God?
A. I am the Son of God, but I have many Brethren.
Q. Have any called thee by the name of Jesus?
A. Not as unto the visible, but as Jesus, the Christ that is in me . . . .
Q. By whom were you sent?
A. By him who hath sent the spirit of his Son in me to try, not as to carnal matters, but belonging to the Kingdom of God, by the indwelling of the Father and the Son, by judge of all spirits to be guided by none.
Q. Is not the written word of God the guide?
A. The written word declares of it, and what is not according to, that is not true.
Q. Whether art thou more sent then others, or whether others be not sent in that measure?
A. As to that I have nothing at present given me of my Father to answer . . . .
Q. How dost thou provide for a lively hood?
A. As do the Lillies without care, being maintained by my father.
Q. Who dost thou call Father?
A. He whom thou callest God.[1]

Fox made no attempt to frame a system of doctrine, and the background of much of the Quaker teaching seems to

[1] John Deacon, *The Grand Impostor Examined; or, The Life, Tryal and Examination of James Naylor.* . . . (London, 1656), pp. 11-15.

have been the accepted theology of the day. In Isaac Penington, the younger,[1] and in Nayler there is a mystical doctrine of God, while in Robert Barclay, the great apologist of Quakerism, there is a definite Calvinistic background. The implications of the Quaker doctrine and the theological questions involved will be dealt with in the next chapter.

A religious movement which carried the mystical position of the Seekers to extremes both in doctrine and conduct was that of Ranterism. How widespread the Ranters were is hard to determine, but in 1651 a judge told George Fox, the founder of the Quakers, that but for the Quakers the Ranters would have overrun the nation.[2] The Quakers in particular were disturbed by the Ranters both in England and America. Richard Baxter attempted to relate them to other movements of the time, and distinguished two kinds of Ranters, the first those of " greater sobriety ". These were

but few, and men of commendable parts, who are deeply possessed with the fancies of Jacob Behmen, the German Paracelsian prophet, and the Rosicrusians, and set themselves mainly to a mortification of bodily desires and delights, and advancing the intellective part above the sensitive (which is well), but the doctrines of Christ crucified and justification by faith is little minded of them. They do, as the quakers, maintain the popish doctrine of perfection, that they can live without sin, or that some of them can. They aspire after a visible communion with angels, and many of them pretend to have attained it, and frequently to see them. The rest have that immediate intuition of verities by the Spirit within them, or by revelation, that is above mere rational apprehension, and therefore they will not dispute, nor be moved by any argument of scriptures that you

---

[1] Isaac Penington (1616-1679), eldest son of Sir Isaac Penington, Lord Mayor of London. The younger Penington became a Quaker in 1657. He wrote several theological treatises.

[2] *The Journal of George Fox*, p. 52.

bring, affirming that ratiocination cannot prevail against their intuition.[1]

The Ranters seem to have carried a pantheistic mysticism to logical conclusions. In a tract marked by occasional beauty of expression and apparent depth of religious feeling, Jacob Bauthumley wrote of the "Light and Dark Side of God." One side of God is the series, God, heaven, earth; the other side is the series, devil, sin, hell. God does not have his being in one place more than in another; he is " in all Creatures, Man and Beast, Fish and Fowle, and every green thing, from the highest Cedar to the Ivey on the wall." Man only carries " a more lively image of the divine Being than any other Creature ". The reason men use set times of prayer and tend toward "formal duties " is that they conceive of God as " locally " in heaven and as remaining in one place.[2]

In the only surviving document known to present the spiritual autobiography of a Ranter, Joseph Salmon, who seems to have been at one time imprisoned for blasphemy, publishes a recantation; but beneath the orthodox phrases the Ranter trend is evident. " Every thing beares a constant greedy motion toward the center; and when once we are wearied in the prolixity of variety, we revolve into silence, where we are as if we had never been." [3]

According to John Holland some Ranters declared the Scriptures to be " a dead Letter," a bundle of contradictions, the cause of all the blood that has been shed in the world, and that he had heard one claim that he had the spirit of

[1] Baxter, *Practical Works*, vol. ii, p. 349.

[2] Jacob Bauthumley, *The Light and Dark Sides of God: or a plain and brief Discourse of the light side—God, Heaven, and Earth; the dark side—Devil, Sin, and Hell. . . .* (London, 1650), pp. 4-7. This tract is in the British Museum, but parts of it are reprinted in Barclay, *op. cit.*

[3] Joseph Salmon, *Heights in Depths and Depths in Heights . . .* (London, 1651), p. 30.

God as much as Paul and that what he wrote was as infallible as what Paul wrote.[1]

Associated with the Ranters were a number of fanatics who made themselves particularly obnoxious to contemporaries. One John Robins, who was called by his opposers "the Ranters' God,"[2] claimed to be God Almighty and to have raised from the dead, Cain, Judas, Jeremiah and others. Lodowick Muggleton, founder of the Muggletonians, was much impressed by Robins and his partner, one Tannye, a Jew. Muggleton records, gravely enough, that he saw all those whom Robins claimed to have raised from the dead "and they owned themselves to be the very same Persons that had been dead for so long a time".[3]

Lodowick Muggleton (1609-1698) was a London tailor, and, in his younger days, a zealous Puritan. He became associated with the two fanatics, Robins and Tannye; but in 1652, Muggleton and his cousin, John Reeves, had visions which convinced them that they were the two prophets mentioned in Revelation XI, who were to stand before the Lord and prophesy. Muggleton seems to have been particularly impressed with the provision that the "witnesses" should curse their enemies, and many of the incidents preserved by Muggleton in his book, *The Acts of the Witnesses of the Spirit,* are hearty, if somewhat indiscriminate condemnations. There seems to have been no rational background for the beliefs of Muggleton, and the idea of God held by

[1] John Holland, *The Smoke of the Bottomlesse Pit* .... (London, 1651), p. 4. The British Museum copy has a manuscript correction of the date, substituting the year 1650; but in the catalogue of the Thomason Tracts 1651 is retained.

[2] William Charles Braithwaite, *The Second Period of Quakerism,* p. 22. Cf. *The Ranters' Creed* ... (London, 1651), an account of John Robins' trial.

[3] Lodowick Muggleton, *The Acts of the Witnesses of the Spirit* (London 1699), p. 21.

the witnesses was so anthropomorphic that William Penn speaks of Muggleton's " six-foot God ".[1]

Thus far the sects and individuals whose doctrine and conduct have been described, have been of the seventeenth century and mainly of the four decades following the Long Parliament. But enthusiastic claims did not cease with the coming of William III and middle-class " common sense ". At the beginning of the new century a group of refugees from the Cevennes in France arrived in London, and the pamphleteers renewed their battle over immediate inspiration.

The Revocation of the Edict of Nantes in 1685 led to an uprising in the Cevennes which for a time attained the proportions of civil war. Savage repression of a religious people was followed by outbreaks of prophetism, and there were said to have arisen as many as five or six hundred prophets in less than a year from June 1688.[2] In the land which, a generation before, had been moved at the thought of

> . . . slaughtered Saints, whose bones
> Lie scattered on the Alpine Mountains cold,

there was much sympathy for the persecuted Protestants. The " prophets " who came to England made some converts even among the wealthy and well-born: it is plain that opponents were much annoyed at the adherence in England of men like Sir Richard Bulkeley and John Lacey.[3]

---

[1] Muggleton, *The Acts of the Witnesses of the Spirit,* p. 125. Jessop has a charming essay on " The Prophet of Walnut-Tree Yard " in his *The Coming of the Friars and other Historical Essays* (London, 1913).

[2] On the Camisards *vide* J. B. Cutten, *Speaking with Tongues;* R. Heath, " The Little Prophets of the Cevennes ", *Contemporary Review,* Jan. 1886; H. M. Baird, " The Camisard Uprising," *Papers of the American Society of Church History,* vol. ii, pt. i; Theophilus Evans, *The History of Modern Enthusiasm,* Second Edition (London, 1757); M. de Brueys, *Histoire du Fanatisme de Notre tems.* . . . (Utrecht, 1737).

[3] *Cf. Enthusiastick Impostors no Divinely Inspired Prophets.* . . (London, 1707), " Dedication."

The prophets predicted the restoration of mankind to primitive beauty and purity and the pouring out of the Spirit upon all who should desire it. There were attempted healings [1] and an active propaganda was carried on by emissaries who claimed to be inspired while in abnormal states. " Among much more than a thousand Ecstasys that I have seen ", wrote Sir Richard Bulkeley, " I have seen many, so very much agitated and mov'd that no part could be said to be in Repose; as if they had been stomach-sick, Heart-sick, Fainting, rack'd with cholicks Stone and Gout." [2]

The French prophets lost much of their popularity when they failed to raise a dead man in Bunhill Fields in 1708, but John Lacy was committed to Bridewell as late as 1737, and in 1738 Charles Wesley slept with a follower of the prophets, who, while they were undressing, " fell into violent agitations, and gobbled like a turkey-cock ". Wesley exorcised him, but passed a restless night " with Satan so near ".[3]

[1] *Vide* especially John Lacy, *A relation of the Dealings of God to his unworthy servant John Lacy.* . . . (London, 1708).

[2] Sir Richard Bulkeley, *An Answer to Several Treatises Lately Published on the Subject of the Prophets. The First Part.* . . . (London, 1708), pp. 35-6. On the propaganda of the French Prophets, *vide* preface to Henry Nicholson, *The Falshood of the New Prophets Manifested with their corrupt Doctrine and conversations.* . . . (London, 1708).

[3] *The Journal of the Rev. Charles Wesley, M.A.* . . . (reprint of 1849 edition of Thomas Jackson), Dec. 11, 1738, vol. i, p. 138.

CHAPTER III

Theological Controversies

One needs hardly to be told that the religious disturbances of the period from the Great Rebellion to the rise of Methodism are reflected in theological literature. Indeed, if theologians were not proverbially controversial, the seriousness of the doctrinal questions involved in claims to immediate inspiration would have compelled careful consideration by all who were concerned for the foundations of Christianity; for the problem of ultimate religious authority was posed by every enthusiast, even though he were innocent of all theology. Is this ultimate religious authority to be found in the Church, in the scriptures, in something called Reason, or in the immediate deliverance of the Holy Spirit? And involved as corollaries are questions concerning learning, order and morality.

The word, enthusiasm, was not confined by the seventeenth century to Greek usage. Most writers employed it as a synonym for false claims to inspiration and without regard to any distinction between mystical experience and that divine seizure which was originally designated by the word.

Opponents of different theological complexion agreed in certain general condemnations of enthusiasm, which conflicted in theory with accepted notions as to the manner of the Christian revelation. Thomas Comber (1645-1699), dean of Durham, contended that the gospel came in a definite, historical manner, and must be learned in a specific, rational manner. Such a historical revelation can not be reconciled with the theory that the gospel has been and is now revealed to the individual through the indwelling Christ, or Spirit, or divine essence.[1] Such a claim rests upon a misunderstanding as to how the Apostles learned the gospel. They learned it from Jesus, the Son of Mary, the Word, and not from the Spirit. If the Spirit helped, it was but to pursue Christ's teachings, or to persuade men of what they knew of their own personal knowledge, to call matters to their remembrance, or to open such things as they did not understand.[2] The gospel in its original was authenticated by miracles, by the audible voices from heaven and by " the punctual fulfilling in Christs Person, Doctrines, Life, Death, &c. what had by a Series of Prophets several hundred years before been predicted concerning him ".[3]

The Revelation once for all committed would not be reopened, although a new revelation as to particular duties, events or matters of fact was possible.[4] Some went so far as to indicate some probable cases of modern revelation. Samuel Rutherford, a Scottish Presbyterian divine who was one of the commissioners of the Church of Scotland to the Westminster Assembly, distinguished in scholastic form four sorts of revelation: 1. prophetic; 2. special revelations to elect only; 3. revelation of some facts to godly men; 4. false and satanical revelations. The first kind was to the pen-men of the Scriptures; the second assures the elect that

[1] As Francis Bugg phrased it: " It was not the Light within which was hanged on a Tree." *The Picture of Quakerism* (London, 1697), p. 23.

[2] Comber, *op. cit.*, chap. ii. For contemporary views concerning the inspiration of the Scriptures, *vide* H. Watkin-Jones, *The Holy Spirit from Arminius to Wesley* (London, pref. 1928), chap. viii.

[3] *Ibid.*, " Epistle to the Reader."

[4] Richard Baxter, *A Christian Directory,* part iii, " Christian Ecclesiastics," answer to question clx, *The Practical Works of Richard Baxter,* vol. i, p. 722.

they are the chosen of God; the third was the revelation of certain things to Wyclif, Luther and others.[1]

Seventeenth-century High Churchmen were inclined to follow scholastic formulations and to distinguish the operations of the Spirit as ordinary and extraordinary. George Hickes (1642-1715), a High Churchman and, after the Revolution, a nonjuring bishop, set forth this distinction at length in *The Spirit of Enthusiasm Exorcised,* a sermon preached before the University of Oxford Sunday, July 11, 1680. He followed Thomas Aquinas in his division of spiritual gifts. The ordinary gifts, *gratiae gratum facientes,* are such as faith, hope, charity, humility; extraordinary gifts, *gratiae gratis datae,* are such as the gift of tongues, the power of working miracles and prophecies. The ordinary gifts are but " moral vertues insensibly wrought in our hearts by the Holy Ghost, we ourselves co-operating therewith ". The extraordinary gifts are either " pure intellectual habits ", as the gift of tongues or the discerning of spirits, or " bodily virtues and powers ", as the power of healing. These " virtues " might make one a more eminent man or minister, " yet was he not made a better Christian than he was before ". As to the extent of these extraordinary gifts, they are not given to all churches nor to the same church in all conditions. When they are given, they are given to " Ministers more than to the people, to children not at all, and seldomer to women than to men ". The Apostles had these special gifts, the gift of tongues, for example, being necessary for the propagation of the gospel; but Christians since the days of the Apostles have generally received only the common gifts of the Spirit.[2]

[1] Samuel Rutherford, *A Survey of the Spiritual Antichrist,* pt. i, chap. vii.

[2] George Hickes, *The Spirit of Enthusiasm Exorcised* (London, 1680), pp. 4-7.

While agreeing in these condemnations of enthusiasm, another group approached the problem with the presuppositions of Platonists. John Smith (1618-1652), fellow of St. John's College, Cambridge, and friend of Benjamin Whichcote, Henry More and the other so-called Cambridge Platonists, wrote a brief, learned treatise " of Prophesie . . .", in which, with much display of his acquaintance with the Jewish commentators and rabbis, he discussed the whole question of prophetic inspiration.[1] In general, Smith agrees with his fellow-churchmen. Prophecy ceased in the Christian church at least after the second century; and an inspiration must be authenticated to others either by similar inspiration or by miracle. But there are some points in Smith's argument which are plainly from the Platonic stratum of his thought.

The true prophetical spirit is seated in the rational as well as in the sensitive powers; and this spirit never alienates the mind, but informs and enlightens it. True, the prophet is often stirred deeply by his vision, so that the impressions by which the prophets received the inspiration " carried a strong evidence of their Original along with them ";[2] but the element of rationality is always there.

For the full solution of this knot we have before shewed how this Pseudo-prophetical Spirit only flutters below upon the more terrene parts of mans Soul, his Passions and Phansie. The Prince of darkness comes not within the Sphere of Light and Reason to order affairs there, but that is left to the sole Oeconomy and Soveraignty of the Father of Lights . . .[3]

Besides miracles, prophesies may be attested by their rea-

---

[1] Dean Inge has an amiable appreciation of Smith in his *The Platonic Tradition in English Religious Thought* (London, 1926), pp. 58-64. On the Cambridge Platonists, *vide infra*, pp. 84-89. The treatise, "On Prophesie," is printed in *Select Discourses . . . By John Smith . . .* (London, 1660), pp. 167-280.

[2] *Select Discourses*, p. 206.

[3] *Ibid.*, p. 203.

sonableness, and this is the method which the latitudinarian writer prefers:

> And I wish this last way of becoming acquainted with Divine Truth were better known amongst us: For when we have once attained to a true sanctified frame of Mind, we have then attained to the End of all Prophesie, and see all divine Truth that tends to the salvation of our Souls in the Divine light, which alwaies shines in the Puritie & Holiness of the New Creature, and so need no further Miracle to confirm us in it.[1]

A major issue in the theological controversy was the authority of the Scriptures. A sure test of the authenticity of any revelation is to be found in the Scriptures. Richard Baxter has an argument which resembles the famous remark about the advisability of destroying the Alexandrian library. If a revelation is contrary to the Scriptures, says Baxter, then the revelation must be rejected; if the revelation agrees with Scripture, it is unnecessary. If it be "besides the Scripture," it must be proven by self-attesting power to one who has it, and to others by miracles and prophecy.[2]

This supremacy of Scripture the enthusiast would not grant. The Quaker apologist, Robert Barclay,[3] maintained that the knowledge of Scripture is not necessary for salvation and cited the cases of deaf people, children and idiots, in proof. He added instances of unlearned people who refused to accept certain readings of the English translation of

[1] *Select Discourses,* pp. 266-7.

[2] *Christian Directory,* part iii, "Christian Ecclesiastics," answer to q. clxiv, *Practical Works,* vol. i, pp. 723-4.

[3] Robert Barclay (1648-1690) was a Scot and had been reared under strict Calvinistic instruction. He was sent to the Scottish Theological Seminary in Paris, where he learned French and Latin. He was received in high circles even after he became a Quaker in 1667. His *Apology for the true Christian Divinity,* which was first published in 1676, is the standard theological work of the Quakers. The edition quoted here is the "Stereotype Edition" (Philadelphia, 1908).

the Bible because the readings disagreed " with the Manifestation of truth in their hearts ", and who were right in their refusal, as Barclay had later found on examining the passages in the original. Canonicity can only be ascertained from inward assurance and Barclay calls attention to questions which make other criteria difficult, such as the questions about authorship in the case of books like Peter, James, II and III John and Revelation; about different readings in the Hebrew and Greek; and about " errors which may be supposed by the injury of time to have slipped in." [1] The Spirit, Barclay concludes, is the guide " which neither moths nor time can wear out, nor transcribers nor translators corrupt." [2] Underneath all assumptions of authority in religion lies the assumption of the final authority of the Spirit. The papists hold to the authority of the church and of tradition; but the church is supposed to be led by an infallible spirit, and tradition was delivered by doctors and fathers who acted by revelation. Protestants and Socinians make the Scriptures the final court of appeal, Protestants " as subjectively influenced by the Spirit to use them ", the Socinians " as managing them with and by their own Reason "; but both Protestants and Socinians trust the Scriptures because the mind of God is thought to have been revealed to the sacred writers. The ultimate authority, therefore, is the Holy Spirit.[3]

The Reformed doctrine of the testimony of the Holy Spirit was adduced in reply to the enthusiasts, but Milton in using this comes near the doctrine he opposes:

Under the gospel we possess, as it were, a twofold Scripture: one external, which is the written word, and the other internal,

[1] Barclay, *Apology*, proposition iii, section iv.
[2] *Ibid.*
[3] *Ibid.*, proposition ii, section xvi.

which is the Holy Spirit, written in the hearts of believers, according to the promise of God. Hence, although the external ground which we possess for our belief at the present day in the written word is highly important, and in most instances, at least, prior in point of reception, that which is internal, and the peculiar possession of each believer, is far superior to all, namely, the Spirit himself.[1]

Writers more orthodox, or less independent than Milton guarded their statements so as to save the authority of the Scriptures. " The Spirit is not given to make our religion reasonable," wrote Baxter, " but to make sinners reasonable, in habit and act, for the believing it." [2] The Spirit, said Baxter, is not the " objective " cause of belief but the " efficient " cause. The Spirit works on man to cause him to believe nothing but what is credible.[3] Rutherford would not bow down before an " inke-Divinity, and meere paper-godlinesse," for the written directions of a physician do not help the sick man, if those directions remain in the sick man's pocket; but while the " strengthening physical power " by which men act is from the Spirit " that worketh with the word," the " obliging power " itself is from the Scriptures. The Spirit as the Spirit is not a moral rule for men to act by but is to be followed when the Spirit goes with the Law and the testimony, for only then does the believer know that the Spirit is of God.[4]

Another consequence of enthusiasm, in the eyes of the theologians, was the substitution of the authority of immediate inspiration for the authority of the church and its ministry. Edmund Calamy (1671-1732), a prominent non-

---

[1] John Milton, *A Treatise on Christian Doctrine.* . . . trans. by Charles R. Summers (Cambridge, 1825), p. 475.

[2] *The Unreasonableness of Infidelity,* preface, *Practical Works,* vol. ii, p. 245.

[3] *Ibid.*

[4] Rutherford, *A Survey of the Spiritual Antichrist,* pt. i, p. 304.

conformist minister, gave as one of the characteristics of enthusiasm: inveighing against the recognized ministry of the church.[1] The enthusiastic sects were not only dissenters from the Establishment but also from centralized ecclesiastical authority of other kinds. The Quaker allowed no ordained ministry or ecclesiastical officers, and the more radical sects were markedly anti-ecclesiastical. Here was the old antagonism of prophet against elder which was fought out in Montanism. In this practice, the enthusiasts were as offensive to Dissent as to the Establishment. Luther and Calvin had been insistent upon the call of the church as necessary to a valid ministry, and upon the authorized preaching of the Word as a mark of the true church. Anything that looked toward church control was opposed by the enthusiasts, and with this went depreciation of a learned ministry.

In the controversy over a learned ministry, dependence upon the Spirit's teaching was exalted by some who would not at all dispense with the Scriptures. In 1640 a sermon preached by a Baptist cobbler preacher, Samuel How, was published under the title: *The Sufficiencie of the Spirits Teaching, Without Humane Learning. Or, a Treatise, Tending to Prove Humane Learning to be no Help to the Spirituall Understanding of the Word of God . . . Seen, Allowed, and Printed* . . . (1640). This was republished in 1644 and 1655; the eighth edition appeared in 1781. How was described by Roger Williams as " that eminent Christian witness, and prophet of Christ . . . who being by calling a cobler, and without human learning, which yet in its sphere and place he honoured, who yet, I say, by searching the Holy Scriptures, grew so excellent a textuary or scripture learned man, that few of those high Rabbis that scorn to mend or make a shoe, could aptly or readily from the Holy Scriptures out-go him." He died in prison in 1640, and

[1] Edmund Calamy, *A Caveat against New Prophets*, p. 47.

having been excommunicated was buried in the highway.[1] The burden of How's contention was that the unlearned are more likely to receive the Spirit's aid in understanding than are the learned. Learning, which he defines as " knowledge of the Arts and Sciences, divers Tongues, and such reading," [2] is fit for " states-men, Physicians, Lawyers and Gentlemen," [3] but is like fire, to be kept in the chimney, that is, for worldly employment. The Spirit of God is recognized by its agreement with the witness of the Word and by its operation or works.[4]

How's contention was thus not so much for immediate inspiration as for help in understanding the Scriptures; the argument was carried further by enthusiasts. In 1646, the author of *A Vindication of Learning* . . . refutes a more radical doctrine which had been preached in the " Tower Church by a young Preacher of very good parts, & shew of learning ", a teaching which had " growne Epidemical among the Sectaries and some others that professe learning within the City of London." [5] This writer complains that " many illiterate men in this imaginarie age of Revelations having no outside calling thereunto, but presuming upon their gifts and inward calling, (as they suppose) take upon them not only to censure learning and learned men, but also to Expound, Preach, and deliver the Word of God to the people, assuming unto themselves the power and operations of the holy Ghost, gifts of Prophesie and Revelation. . . ." [6]

[1] R. W. Dale, *History of English Congregationalism* (London, 1907), p. 361.

[2] *The Sufficiencie of the Spirits Teaching,* p. B, b.

[3] *Ibid.,* p. C 4, b.

[4] *Ibid.,* p. E 2.

[5] *A Vindication of Learning From Unjust Aspersions.* . . . (London, 1646), p. 2.

[6] *Ibid.,* p. 25.

THEOLOGICAL CONTROVERSIES

The controversy was precipitated into the Universities by William Dell, Master of Gonville and Caius College, Cambridge, in a sermon which he preached at St. Mary's, Cambridge, in 1653. Dell claimed that " the word of Christ cannot be learned as humane Arts and Sciences can, to wit by the teaching of man, together with their own pains and endeavors, but only by the teaching of God and his Spirit. . ."[1] " The Gospel of Christ, understood according to Aristotle, hath begun, continued, and perfected the mysterie of Iniquity in the outward Church."[2] This was answered by Joseph Sedgwick in a sermon also preached at St. Mary's. The Apostles did receive knowledge in an extraordinary manner, but this was " by way of supply to their illiterate education ".[3] The Spirit could reveal the mind of God immediately " even now as formerly ", but " the Apostles have already delivered the mind of God and the truths of the Gospel: now they are to be read, to be inquired into and meditated upon ".[4] Former methods have ceased. " Manna was in the Wilderness, but Bread must be made in the land of Canaan, where it may be made. . . . Up and be getting for your selves; seek the Lord in the present way of his discovery, and affect not the lazy vanity of immediate illapses."[5] Many acquired gifts are in substance the same as those formerly conferred by the Spirit; these are truly " gifts " of the Spirit, although they are not miraculously acquired.[6] Sedgwick elsewhere lumps enthusiasm with use-

---

[1] William Dell, *The Stumbling-Stone* (London, 1653), p. 16.

[2] Dell, *A Plain and Necessary Confutation of Divers gross and Antichristian Errors delivered . . . . By Mr. Sydrach Sympson* (London, 1654), " An Apologie to the Reader ".

[3] *A Sermon Preached at St. Marie's . . . Or, An Essay to the discovery of the Spirit of Enthusiasme and pretended Inspiration that disturbs and strikes at the Universities* (London, 1653), p. 14.

[4] *Ibid.*, p. 13.

[5] *Ibid.*, p. 14. [6] *Ibid.*, p. 54.

less " philosophy " as inferior " to genuine Philosophy proceeding upon true principles of nature, i.e. God's discovery of himself to our understandings by the light of Reason and Works of Creation." [1]

This controversy can not here be followed in detail since certain aspects of it will be noticed in a succeeding chapter. But as Sedgwick's work indicates the relation of experimental science to enthusiasm, a work by Joseph Glanvill (1636-1680), a clergyman and a member of the Royal Society, may be quoted as suggesting one reason for the position taken by the latitudinarians, who sought to shorten the line defended by fellow churchmen by reducing religion to certain tenets which were supposedly reasonable and easy of demonstration. Glanvill, in his *Reasonable Recommendation* . . . (London, 1670), declared " sickly conceits, and Enthusiasticke dreams, and unsound doctrines " to be the " Fountains of the great Deeps of Atheism, and Fanaticism, that are broken upon us." [2] To meet these, he proposed the reduction of religion to the fundamentals of Decalogue and Creed.[3] Reason is innate ideas,[4] from which all other ideas are derived; consequently men may hold erroneous opinions from a mistaken sense of Scripture and yet not err in faith.[5]

The reduction of religion to that which may be rationally demonstrated was carried a step farther by the writers who are usually classed together, somewhat loosely, as deists. If the orthodox theologians had confined miracles and immediate revelation to a certain historic period, the deists ques-

[1] *The Use of Learning.* . . . (1653), p. 55. James Bass Mullinger quotes this in his *The University of Cambridge,* vol. iii, p. 451, as reflecting the influence of the nascent Royal Society.

[2] *Reasonable Recommendation and Defence of Reason.* . . . pp. 148-9.

[3] *Ibid.,* pp. 214-5.

[4] *Ibid.,* pp. 161-2.

[5] *Ibid.,* pp. 212-14.

tioned them altogether. The controversy between rationalistic theologians and deistic writers was over the sufficiency of natural religion. Matthew Tindal argued that God did not give " positive " law in religion, but that he gave only the law of nature, which is discerned by reason. Otherwise there would be changes in the mind of God and therefore endless revelations.[1]

According to the deist, any appeal to authority which weakens " the force of demonstration " weakens religion. A claim " that God revealed his will by visions, dreams, trances, or any other way except by the light of nature, can only come under the head of probability. And, if it be but probable, that God made any external revelation at all, it can be but probable, though perhaps not in the same degree of probability, that he made this, or that revelation." [2]

Since it was only in the extent to which external revelation was allowed that the deist differed from the " supernatural rationalists ",[3] the deist could say truly enough: " Divine Faith is either when God speaks to us immediately himself, or when we acquiesce in the Words of those to whom we believe he has spoken. All Faith now in the World is of this last sort, and by consequence entirely built upon Ratiocination." [4] Such a state of mind among the theologians made it possible for the deists, who went farther than their more orthodox brethren, practically to ignore the possibility of enthusiasm. "All our divine reasonings about divine revelation are necessarily gathered by our natural no-

[1] *Christianity as Old as the Creation: or the Gospel a Republication of the Religion of Nature* (Newburgh, 1798), pp. 115-17. The first edition was published at London in 1735.

[2] *Ibid.*, p. 159.

[3] *Cf.* A. C. McGiffert, *Protestant Thought Before Kant* (New York, 1915), p. 199 *et seq.*

[4] John Toland, *Christianity not Mysterious* (London, 1702), p. 127.

tions about religion", wrote Tindal, "and therefore, he, who sincerely desires to do the will of God, is not apt to be imposed upon by vain, and confident pretences of divine revelation. . . ." [1]

The rationalism of eighteenth-century divines who had drunk deeply of deistical talk of the law of nature may be illustrated by William Warburton, Bishop of Gloucester (1698-1779). In his *Doctrine of Grace,* Warburton expounds Paul's doctrine of the gifts of the Spirit, as these gifts are enumerated in I Cor. XII. The "word of wisdom" is "all the great principles of natural religion". "Faith" is that faith which is attended with the power of controlling nature. The gift of healing is "that salutary assistance administered to the sick, in a solemn office of the church, as directed by St. James". The gift of miracles is "a more private and extemporaneous exercise of the same power, though less confined in its object". Prophecy signifies foretelling the future of the church, "to the comfort and edification . . . of the assembly". Lastly, the gift of discerning spirits is a gift of testing, or in Warburton's verbose style, "of distinguishing between true and false inspiration, where accidental ambiguity or designed imposture had made the matter doubtful or suspected." [2]

In an elaborate argument, Warburton sought to prove from such passages as I Corinthians XIII. 8, that miraculous gifts were intended to pass away with the first ages of the church.[3] The church needed them at first, since the minds of the Apostles were "rude and uninformed; strangers to

[1] *Vide, Christianity as Old as Creation,* pp. 184-190.

[2] William Warburton, *The Doctrine of Grace; or, The Office and Operations of the Holy Spirit Vindicated from the Insults of Infidelity and the Abuse of Fanaticism.* . . . (1750), in *The Works of the Right Reverend William Warburton, D.D., Lord Bishop of Gloucester* (London, 1811), vol. viii, pp. 264-265.

[3] *Ibid.,* p. 307 *et seq.*

all celestial knowledge; prejudiced in favour of a carnal law, and utterly averse to the genius of the everlasting Gospel."[1] The conditions which demanded these gifts have passed away; and any pretence of them must be tried by the Scriptures and by the tests given there for such trial.[2]

The quandary into which enthusiasm led the church was not only theoretical but practical. Edmund Calamy, writing against the French Prophets, selected as some of the characteristics of enthusiasts " from one Age to another: " expecting to be believed without proof, spiritual pride and a greater dependence upon " their own Whimsies, than on the Sacred Oracles.[3] The qualities of an enthusiast are set forth by another writer as ambition, ignorance and weakness of mind (often also weakness of body), and venting supposed revelations without regard to ecclesiastical discipline. To these qualities of enthusiasm are added the more ordinary results of enthusiasm, thinking it well to pray continually, expectation of special assistance from God " in all emergent difficulties," running into extremes, yielding blind obedience to the irregular motions of a diseased brain, frequent changes from joy to despair.[4] The enthusiasts were obnoxious because they acted " by motions, not by motives."[5]

The acceptance of impulses to action as authoritative commands from God made for a more intense individualism than did mysticism; and while some, like Fox, might find unity for their disparate impulses in an experience of unity and

[1] Warburton, *op. cit.*, p. 317.
[2] *Ibid.*, pp. 320, 321.
[3] Edmund Calamy, *A Caveat against New Prophets*, p. 47.
[4] Henry Wharton, *The Enthusiasm of the Church of Rome demonstrated in some observations upon the life of Ignatius Loyola* (London, 1688), pp. 20-98 *passim*.
[5] Comber, *Christianity no Enthusiasm*, p. 5.

peace, the danger of uncontrolled individualism could not be evaded. This danger was made the more pressing by the common acceptance of current notions of human nature. The doctrine of the corrupt nature of man was commonly believed. A man could not be expected to have of himself any good thought or to do any good action, " for whatsoever real good any man doth, it proceedeth not from his nature, as he is man, or the son of Adam; but from the seed of God in him . . . so that, though it be in him, yet it is not of him." [1] Every impulse which seemed good was liable, therefore, to appraisal as the moving of the Holy Spirit.[2] In the theology of the day inspiration was linked with infallibility. William Penn was at one with most of his age in being unable to imagine an inspiration that is not infallible:

What, make that heresy, which is the root of all true religion? as well true ministry? Can a fallible spirit bring people into the truth, or turn them to God? Is not the spirit of God an infallible Spirit? And are not the children of God led by it? [3]

The enthusiastic sects had broken with the churches, and were therefore without effective social control. Need of some sort of discipline was soon felt not only by churchmen but by those sympathetic with enthusiasm. From the beginning the Quakers insisted that no impulse was divine which led to immoral actions. To the question whether a man should be free to follow his inner persuasion, William

[1] Barclay, *Apology,* proposition iv, section i.
[2] See Braithwaite, *Spiritual Guidance in the Experience of the Society of Friends* (London, 1909), p. 34 *et seq.* Mr. Braithwaite's article "Friends, Society of ..." in the *Encyclopedia of Religion and Ethics,* gives a good short statement of the problems involved in the attempt made by Barclay and others to formulate Quaker doctrine with a background of Calvinistic theology. See also Introduction by Professor R. M. Jones to Braithwaite, *Second Period of Quakerism,* p. xxxii *et seq.*
[3] William Penn, *The New Athenians no Noble Bereans,* in *Select Works* (London, 1782), vol. iv, p. 469.

Penn answered: "This is true in a sense; that is, if thou art such an one that canst do nothing against the truth, but for the truth, then mayest thou safely be left to thy freedom in the things of God."[1] In 1652, when Fox was troubled with the tendency of the Friends to indulge in "prophesyings," or spontaneous exhortations, he suggested another test for the Spirit's movings:

> To speak of truth, when ye are moved, it is a cross to the will; if ye live in the truth which ye speak, ye live in the cross to your own wills. For that which joins with the earthly will, goes out from God and from that which is pure, and so makes a place for the enchanter and sorcerer and the airy spirit to lodge in.[2]

In other words, only those impulses were to be obeyed that were contrary to the inclinations of the individual. But such a test put a premium upon wayward impulses sufficiently absurd to shock the sensibilities of the person conscious of them, and the application of this test may have been responsible for many of the extravagances into which certain Quakers fell at various times.

More effective criteria than the ordinary rules of morality or the disagreement of an impulse with one's inclinations, were felt to be necessary in order to preserve believers from extravagances which appeared in the uncertain days of the Rebellion and of the Commonwealth. The Quakers, to achieve this, even went so far with their critics as to lay down as a rule: "That whatsoever any do, pretending to the Spirit, which is contrary to the scripture, be accounted and reckoned a delusion of the devil."[3]

The need of social control over vagrant spontaneities of

---

[1] Penn, *A Brief Examination and State of Liberty Spiritual*, in *Works*, vol. iv, p. 283.

[2] Quoted by Braithwaite, *Spiritual Guidance*, pp. 55-6.

[3] Barclay, *Apology*, proposition iii, section vi.

the individual compelled the beginnings of organization among the Quakers. This first rudimentary organization was for the purpose of carrying on charitable work and attending to the ordinary business of a religious group, but there soon emerged the problem of adjusting the claims of the individual to the demands of the group. The controversies within the Quaker ranks and the consequent schisms of the early period of the Friends arose over the problem. There were some who protested against the exercise of authority by the group, and insisted that the true precept is: " Draw water out of your own wells." [1] The Quakers who believed in some type of group control held that

> There never will nor can be wanting in Case of controversie, the Spirit of God to give Judgment through some or other in the Church of Christ, so long as any assembly can properly, or in any tolerable Supposition, be so termed.[2]

Revelation is ordinarily made to the elders and ministers of the church, or to the general meeting. Barclay attempts to defend this apparent aristocracy of inspiration, but he will not say that the individual ought to submit before he is " clear " in the matter. Later, Barclay found it necessary to explain that he did not mean that every group which calls itself Christian will have the infallible spirit, but that he referred only to those groups which have correct doctrines and in which the true life and powers are felt and known. Quakerism was going the way of similar groups; the infallible spirit was being confined to offices and orthodoxies.[3]

The student who surveys the controversy over enthusiasm within the fields of theology and church government must be

---

[1] Quoted in Braithwaite, *The Second Period of Quakerism,* pp. 342-3.

[2] Barclay, *Anarchy of the Ranters* (London, 1676), p. 62.

[3] On early Quaker controversies and schisms, *vide* Braithwaite, *The Second Period of Quakerism,* pp. 342-3, and *Spiritual Guidance,* p. 61.

impressed by the comprehensiveness of the discussion: Platonists, deists, Quakers, Latitudinarians, High Churchmen, Presbyterians, mystics, all contend together. Little that was new appeared in arguments of the orthodox, who were embarrassed by two necessities: that of defending revelation in one historic period and of denying it in another; and that of maintaining a theory of human nature which at the very least made enthusiasm a logical explanation of all good impulses. Rationalist theologians and deists, with varying degrees of plausibility, got rid of enthusiasm by denying the divinity of irrationality whether past or present. The enthusiasts themselves did not usually theorize; those who did, like Barclay, were shrewd in attack but weak in defense, building their justification upon current theories of God and of human nature. Their practical experience in group control is instructive enough but attracted little attention outside of their own circles.

No final solution of the problems raised by enthusiasm was reached by the theologians, who rushed into the controversy over the seat of religious authority without having sensed the real difficulty involved in any claim to infallibility whatsoever.

CHAPTER IV

" Philosophy " and Enthusiasm

IN grouping non-theological discussions of enthusiasm in this period in England, especially in that part of it which falls in the seventeenth century, it is convenient to use " philosophical " in the older sense, which includes biological and psychological. An age when most philosophers were also theologians and when High Churchmen and poets as well as scientists belonged to the young Royal Society defies a neat differentiation of " theologians," " philosophers " and " scientists." Theology, experimental science and speculative philosophy have rarely been more confusingly mixed than in seventeenth-century England. Sir Thomas Browne, who wrote against popular errors, believed heartily in witchcraft; Locke accepted the inerrancy of the Scriptures; Newton wrote a cumbrous interpretation of the Prophets; and Boyle gravely discussed the occult virtue of gems.

The agreement of orthodoxy and philosophy is nowhere clearer than in considerations of enthusiasm by some who have gained reputations as destroyers of scholastic idols. If Francis Bacon " more than any other led the world out of the path opened by Aquinas, and into that through which modern thought has advanced to its greatest conquests," [1] his explanation of immediate inspiration gives little evidence of it.

Following Cicero, Bacon recognized two kinds of divina-

---

[1] Andrew D. White, *A History of the Warfare of Science with Theology in Christendom* (N. Y., 1897), vol. i, p. 400.

"PHILOSOPHY" AND ENTHUSIASM

tion, natural and artificial. Natural divination is of two kinds, "native" and "by influx". The mind when "abstracted or collected in itself and not diffused in the organs of the body" has from its natural power some foreknowledge of the future, which appears chiefly in sleep, ecstasies and at the near approach of death. This is "native" divination. Divination by influx is when the mind as a mirror receives "a secondary illumination" from the foreknowledge of God and from spirits. The regime of the body such as abstinence, which is useful in native divination, is helpful also in this kind: " for the same abstraction of the mind causes it more powerfully to use its own nature, and renders it more susceptive to divine influxes, only in divination by influx the soul is seized with a kind of rapture, and as it were impatience of the Deity's presence, which the ancients called by the name of sacred fury, whereas in native divination the soul is rather at its ease and free." [1]

The attitude toward enthusiasm of a learned Englishman in the middle of the seventeenth century may be illustrated by a treatise from the pen of Meric Casaubon (1599-1671), son of the famous Isaac Casaubon, who, although a doctor of divinity, was known principally as a classical scholar. An outspoken royalist, Casaubon was ejected from his living in 1644, but was treated with deserved courtesy by Cromwell and was returned to preferment after the Restoration. He was the author of several works on classical subjects and of a well-known defence of witchcraft. He was not, however, unusually credulous for his time: he advised, for example, against conviction of witches upon their own testimony.

Casaubon's book on immediate inspiration was entitled *A Treatise concerning Enthusiasme, As it is an Effect of*

[1] *The Advancement of Learning*, bk. iv, chap. iii. The edition quoted is that of Creighton (N. Y., c. 1900).

Nature: but is mistaken by many for either Divine Inspiration, or Diabolical Possession . . . (London, 1655). There is such a thing as real enthusiasm, as Casaubon is careful to make clear:

Enthusiasme, say I, is either naturall, or supernaturall. By supernaturall, I understand a true and reall possession of some extrinsecal superior power, whether divine, or diabolical producing effects and operations altogether supernatural: as some kind of divination . . . speaking of strange languages, temporary learning, and the like. By natural Enthusiasme, I understand an extraordinary transcendent, but natural fervency, or pregnancy of the soul, spirits, or brain, producing strange effects, apt to be mistaken for supernatural.[1]

The author's concern is only with this latter kind of enthusiasm. On this point he is meticulously explicit:

But here I meddle not with policy but nature; nor with evil men so much, as the evil consequence of the ignorance of natural causes which both good and evil are subject unto. My business therefore shall be as by examples of all professions in all ages, to shew how men have been very prone upon some grounds of nature, producing some extraordinary though not supernaturale effects; really, not hypocritically, but yet falsely and erroniously, to deem themselves divinely inspired: so secondly to dig and dive (so farre as may be done with warrantable sobriety) into the deep and dark mysteries of nature, for some reasons, and probable confirmations of such natural operations, falsely deemed supernatural.[2]

These careful reservations doubtless express Casaubon's real opinions. He was no time-server, as is evidenced by his refusal of Cromwell's invitation to write a history of the Civil War, on the ground that he would be compelled to say

[1] Casaubon, *Treatise*, p. 17.
[2] *Ibid.*, p. 4.

some unpleasant things about the Protector. But he was writing in what he called " these Anabaptistical times "[1] and on a subject which touched the beliefs of many in power; so it behooved him to be exact.

In this book, enthusiasm is divided into " Divinatory; " " Contemplative and Philosophicall," by which he means mystical ecstasy; " Rhetoricall; " " Poeticall; " and " Precatory," that is praying by inspiration. Although begun by an account of a French mystic, the study concerns itself mainly with classical examples. Nevertheless, the Fathers and contemporaries are not forgotten: " Tertullian had never been an heretick, had he been a better Naturalist; "[2] and Casaubon enlivens his pages with many stories both from modern books and from his own observation.

Enthusiasm is explained on natural grounds, sometimes by a display of shrewd common sense and at other times by employment of current medical theory. The power of orators over their audiences is owing partly to the use of metaphors and allegories, which exercise the imagination, and partly to the musical character of such speech. Fervent prayer is often thought to be inspired because of the vehement intention of the mind at such a time, because of the power of language influencing both speaker and hearer, and because of the natural ardor of certain individuals. As to theoretical explanations, Casaubon is not sure whether enthusiasm is to be ascribed to " a mixture of the elements, and first qualities, in the composition of man, or to some more hidden and remote cause."[3]

It is not possible to follow in detail the curious reasonings by which the natural explanations of various kinds of enthusiasm are attempted. But it must be borne in mind that

[1] Casaubon, *op. cit.*, p. 64.
[2] *Ibid.*, pp. 10-11.
[3] *Ibid.*, p. 17.

in regard to ancient oracles, at least, the devices which Casaubon uses, Aristotelian emanations and the like, are to explain real oracles and real divination. For a good classicist there could be no question of the fact of the ancient oracles, which were so well attested by all the authorities which the humanist most respected; to a Christian, the only supernatural explanation admissible was that these oracles were inspired by demons. The solution was necessarily by some natural explanation which would allow the reality of the prophecies and wonders and yet deny their supernatural character.

In the literature of enthusiasm Casaubon's importance lies in his insistence upon natural causes for enthusiastic phenomena. Nor does he resort to charges of imposture; even Mohammed was not an impostor but an enthusiast.[1] This last is the more notable since both the orthodox and their opponents were assuming that all that was not indubitably supernatural in religion is the result of imposture.

In the *Leviathan,* Thomas Hobbes discussed enthusiasm in its relation to various parts of his arguments. Analyzing intellectual defects he defined madness as the state of a man who has stronger and more vehement passions for anything than is ordinarily seen in others, and he lists pretence to private inspiration as a species of madness. With one eye on the troubles of his native land, Hobbes observed shrewdly that, while the effects of this folly may not be observable in an individual, it is manifest " when many of them conspire together."

Claims to inspiration arise very often " from some lucky finding of an Errour generally held by others; and not knowing, or not remembering, by what conduct of reason, they came to so singular a truth . . . they presently admire themselves; as being in the speciall grace of God Almighty, who

[1] Casaubon, *op. cit.*, pp. 11, 131-2.

hath revealed the same to them supernaturally by his Spirit."[1] Hobbes thinks it strange that the Jews should come into an idea of possession or enthusiasm, since the prophets did not pretend enthusiasm but claimed a voice and command; and he can explain it only by " that which is common to all men; namely, the want of curiosity to search naturall causes; and their placing Felicity, in the acquisition of the grosse pleasures of the Senses, and the things that most immediately conduce thereto."[2] In discussing " the religion of the Gentiles," which he always cautiously differentiates from Christianity, Hobbes attributed enthusiasm to one of the seeds of religion, namely, " Taking of things Casuall for Prognostiques."[3] Among the things casual are " the insignificant Speeches of Madmen, supposed to be possessed with a divine Spirit."[4]

In accordance with his theory of " Common-Wealth ", Hobbes assumed that the founders of states, " among the Gentiles," of course, who designed only to keep the people in obedience and peace, took care to instil belief that precepts taught concerning religion were from God " or other Spirit."[5] He lists, therefore, among " those things that Weaken, or tend to the Dissolution of a Common-wealth " (chap. xxix), the teaching " That Faith and Sanctity, are not to be attained by Study and Reason, but by Supernaturall Inspiration, or Infusion. Which granted," he adds " I see not why any man should render a reason of his Faith; or why

---

[1] *Leviathan Or the Matter, Forme and Power of A Commonwealth Ecclesiasticall and Civill. By Thomas Hobbes of Malmesbury. London. Printed for Andrew Crooke at the Green Dragon in St. Pauls Churchyard*, 1651, part i, chap. 8, p. 36. First folio issue, Wrenn Library copy.

[2] Part i, chap. 8, p. 38.

[3] Part i, chap. 12, p. 54.

[4] Part i, chap. 12, p. 56.

[5] Part i, chap. 12, p. 57.

every Christian should not also be a Prophet; or why any man should take the Laws of his Country, rather than his own Inspiration for the rule of his action." [1] He reiterated his own theology: " Faith comes by hearing, and hearing by those accidents, which guide us into the presence of them that speak to us; which accidents are all contrived by God Almighty; and yet are not supernaturall, but onely, for the great number of them that concurre to every effect, unobservable." [2]

Hobbes' theology, set forth at length in the third part of *Leviathan*, may have been unorthodox in the eyes of contemporaries, but it is agreeable to his materialistic philosophy and to his theory of the state. Parts of it, moreover, are merely the restatement of orthodox positions; while in other parts he anticipates later arguments of the deists.

" Spirit " is simply a word for " either a subtile, fluid, and invisible Body, or a Ghost, or other Idol or Phantasme of the Imagination." [3] Prophecy, which means speaking from God to man, as well as prediction,[4] is not an art, " but an extraordinary, and temporary Employment from God, most often of Good men, but sometimes also of the Wicked." [5] This is true of the " Sovereign Prophets ", of whom Moses and Christ are the great examples; but subordinate prophets spoke only according to God's will as " declared by the supreme Prophet." [6]

Having laid such a foundation, Hobbes proceeded to the main point at which he had been driving in his discussion of revelation. His conclusions may be quoted in full:

[1] Part ii, chap. 29, p. 169.
[2] *Ibid.*
[3] Part ii, chap. 34, p. 208.
[4] Part iii, chap. 36, p. 225.
[5] Part iii, chap. 36, pp. 225-6.
[6] Part iii, chap. 36, p. 229.

Seeing then all Prophecy supposeth Vision, or Dream, (which two, when they be naturall, are the same), or some especiall gift of God, so rarely observed in mankind, as to be admired when observed; And seeing as well such gifts, as the most extraordinary Dreams, and Visions, may proceed from God, not onely by his supernaturall, and immediate, but also by his naturall operation, and by mediation of second causes; there is need of Reason and Judgment to discern between naturall, and supernaturall Gifts, and between naturall, and supernaturall Visions or Dreams. And consequently men had need to be very circumspect, a[n]d wary, in obeying the voice of man, that pretending himself to be a Prophet, requires us to obey God in that way, which he in Gods name telleth us to be the way to happinesse. For he that pretends to teach men the way of so great felicity, pretends to govern them; that is to say, to rule, and reign over them; which is a thing, that all men naturally desire, and is therefore worthy to be suspected of Ambition and Imposture; and consequently, ought to be examined, and tryed by every man, before hee yeeld them obedience; unlesse he have yeelded it them already, in the institution of a Commonwealth; as when the Prophet is the Civill Soveraign, or by the Civil Soveraign Authorized.[1]

The tests to be made of prophecy are the orthodox ones of sound doctrine and miracles,[2] but Hobbes safeguards the latter test to save both man's reason and the authority of the sovereign. Many things seem miraculous only because of their rarity, and what is a miracle to one may not be so to another.[3] A miracle, indeed, is performed only to make manifest the mission of an extraordinary messenger of God. It cannot, then, be performed by a "Devil, Angel, or other created Spirit."[4] Man must give no credit to a pretended

[1] Part iii, chap. 36, p. 230.
[2] Part iii, chap. 36, pp. 231-2.
[3] Part iii, chap. 37, pp. 233-4.
[4] Part iii, chap. 37, p. 235.

miracle or prophet until assured of his doctrine, and this assurance can only come from the "head of the Church." Moreover, after a miracle has been tested, doubtful cases are to be referred to "God's Lieutenant". "A private man has alwaies the liberty, (because thought is free,) to believe, or not beleeve in his heart, those acts that have been given out for Miracles, according as he shall see, what benefit can accrew by mens belief, to those that pretend, or countenance them, and thereby conjecture, whether they be Miracles, or Lies. But when it comes to confession of that faith, the Private Reason must submit to the Publique; that is to say, to Gods Lieutenant."[1] Needless to say, "Gods Lieutenant" is the sovereign.

Hobbes' treatment of enthusiasm is plainly determined by his materialistic philosophy and by his political conceptions. He shrewdly advances reasons for doubting pretenders to inspiration on natural grounds, but there seems no cause to doubt his sincerity when he predicates historical supernatural revelation. His importance in the discussions of immediate inspiration lies in his insistence upon second causes and in his final conclusion, that one may believe a miracle-confirmed revelation without acting upon it or even confessing one's belief.

The classical scholar, Casaubon, and the materialist, Hobbes, may be followed by the Platonist, Henry More (1614-1687).[2] Associated with the Cambridge Platonists, More was affected, especially in his later life, by cabbalistic speculations and devoted much time to interpretation of prophecy. He contended for the existence of immaterial spirits and of witchcraft.

---

[1] Part iii, chap. 37, p. 238.
[2] On More, *vide* John Tulloch, *Rational Theology and Christian Philosophy in England in the Seventeenth Century* (London, 1874), vol. ii, pp. 303-406.

More confessed his own sympathy with the mystics, and Tulloch suggests that he may have disliked fanatical forms of mysticism all the more because he was aware of his own tendencies.[1] In his youth, More had a vision in which an old man gave the young philosopher two keys, on one of which was the inscription, *Claude fenestras ut luceat domus,* and on the other the words, *Amor Dei lux animae.* From this Platonic vision More was recalled to contemporary realities by the braying of two asses which stood beside him.

Nevertheless, More was not discouraged from his inclinations by inclement times, and in middle life wrote: " I must ingenuously confess that I have a natural touch of Enthusiasme in my Complexion, but such as, I thank God, was ever governable enough . . ."[2] His predilection was for the transports of Plato and Plotinus:

> To such Enthusiasm as this, which is but the triumph of the Soul of man, inebriated, as it were, with the delicious sense of the divine life, that blessed Root and Originall of all holy wisedom and vertue, I must declare myself as much a friend, as I am to the vulgar, fanatical Enthusiasm a professed enemy.[3]

He thought that

> there may be such a presage in the spirit of a man that is to act in things of very high concernment to himself, and much more if to the publick, as may be a sure guide to him, especially if he continue constantly sincere, just and pious.[4]

Such is the case

> wherein that of Siriacides may be verified, *That a man's own*

---

[1] Tulloch, *op. cit.,* vol. ii, p. 337.

[2] *A Collection of Several Philosophical Writings of Dr. Henry More,* second edition (London, 1662), Preface, p. x.

[3] More, *Enthusiasmus Triumphatus* (London, 1662), p. 45.

[4] *Ibid.,* p. 21.

heart will tell him more than seven watchmen on an high Tower, But this is Enthusiasm in the better sense, and therefore not so proper for our Discourse: who speak not of that which is true, but of that which is a mistake.[1]

The discourse to which More referred was his *Enthusiasmus Triumphatus; or a Brief Discourse of the Nature, Causes, Kinds and Cure of Enthusiasm* (London, 1656). More defined enthusiasm as "a full, but false perswasion in a man that he is inspired," while real inspiration is "to be moved in an extraordinary manner by the power or Spirit of God to act, speak or think what is holy, just and true.[2]

A false sense of inspiration, or enthusiasm, is attributed to an alteration in the blood and "spirits"; for "our Imagination alters as our Blood and Spirits are altered.[3] More goes into detail in explaining the origin of enthusiasm from the humours in the blood. Wine, for example, will heighten one's temper if not alter it. He relates stories of people who became good mousers after drinking the blood of cats, or who thought themselves to be dogs, wolves, or cats, although they had drunk neither blood nor any "potion." The enthusiast is, in like manner, the victim of a diseased imagination.

The Spirit then that wings the Enthusiast in such a wonderful manner is nothing else but that Flatulency which is in the Melancholy complexion, and rises out of the Hypochondriacal humour upon some occasional heat, as Winde out of the Aeolipila applied to the fire. Which fume mounting into the Head, being first actuated and spirited and somewhat refined by the warmth of the Heart, fills the Mind with variety of Imaginations, and so quickens and inlarges Invention, that it makes the Enthusiast to admiration fluent and eloquent, he being

---

[1] *Op. cit.*, p. 21. More is quoting from *Ecclesiasticus* xxxvii, 14.
[2] *Ibid.*, p. 2. Quotations are from 1662 edition.
[3] *Ibid.*, p. 5.

as it were drunk with new wine drawn from that Cellar of his own that lies in the lowest region of his Body, though he be not aware of it, but takes it to be pure Nectar and those waters of life that spring from above.[1]

The marks of true inspiration are universal piety and goodness; belief in Scripture, particularly in the historic Christ; and prudence preventing anything irrational. More adds certain recommendations for the cure of enthusiasm, the first being temperance:

By Temperance I understand a measurable Abstinence from all hot heightning meats or drinks, as also from all venereous pleasures and tactual delights of the Body, from all softness and effeminacy; a constant and peremptory adhesion of the perfectest degree of Chastity in the single life, and of Continency in wedlock, that can be attained to. For it is plain in sundry examples of Enthusiasm above named, that the more hidden and lurking fumes of Lust had tainted the Phansies of those Pretenders to Prophecy and Inspiration.

We will adde also to these, moderate exercise of the Body and seasonable taking of the fresh aire, and due and discreet use of Devotion, whereby the Blood is ventilated and purged from dark oppressing vapors; which a temperate diet, if not fasting, must also accompany; or else the more hot and zealous our addresses are, the more likely they are to bring mischief upon our own heads, they raising the feculency of our intemperance into those more precious parts of the Body, the Brains and Animal Spirits, and so intoxicating the Mind with fury and wildness.[2]

A soberer writer, who was also associated with the Cambridge Platonists, was Joseph Glanvill (1636-1680).[3] In

[1] More, *op. cit.*, p. 12.

[2] *Ibid.*, p. 37.

[3] On Glanvill, see Lecky, *op. cit.*, vol. i, pp. 129-137; Tulloch, *op. cit.*, vol. ii, pp. 443, 452; Ferris Greenslet, *Joseph Glanvill A Study in English Thought and Letters in the Seventeenth Century* (N. Y., 1900).

his *Philosophia Pia; or, a Discourse of the Religious Temper, and Tendencies of the Experimental Philosophy, which is profest By the Royal Society* . . . (London, 1671), Glanvill devotes part of chapter V to an explanation of the way in which experimental philosophy defends religion against enthusiasm, for claims to immediate inspiration are really crying up diseases and excesses of fancy for heights of godliness:

The real knowledge of Nature detects the dangerous imposture, by shewing what strange things may be effected by no diviner a cause, then a strong fancy impregnated by Heated Melancholy; For this sometimes warms the brain to a degree that makes it very active and imaginative, full of odde thoughts, and unexpected suggestions; so that if the Temper determine the imagination to Religion, it flies at high things, at interpretations of dark and Prophetick Scriptures; at predictions of future events, and mysterious discoveries, which the man expresseth fluently, and boldly, with a peculiar and pathetick eloquence; And now these pregnances being, not ordinary, but much beyond the usual tone, and temper of the Enthusiast; and he having heard great things of the spirits immediate motions and inspirations, cannot well fail of believing himself inspired, and of intitling all the excursions of his fancy to the immediate actings of the Holy Ghost: which thoughts by the help of natural pride, and self-love, will work also exceedingly upon the heightned affections, and they upon the body so far, as to cast it sometimes into raptures, extasies, and deliquiums of sense, in which every dream is taken for a Prophecy, every image of the fancy for a vision, and all the glarings of the imagination, for new Lights, and Revelations.[1]

Glanvill believed that contemporary pretenders were thus moved; they were not imposters, " for they infinitely believe in themselves."[2] Natural philosophy makes men less con-

---
[1] *Philosophia Pia*, pp. 57-59.
[2] *Ibid.*, p. 59.

fident in themselves," [1] frees them from prejudices and " preingagements ",[2] and teaches them " to state matters clearly, and to draw out those conclusions that are lodged in them." [3]

This defence of natural philosophy must not be taken too seriously, for while it pointed in the right direction, it was capable of many interpretations. The Reason which man uses is deduction from certain innate principles,[4] and it may be employed to defend many things. Glanvill's book, *Sadducismus Triumphatus,* was thought by Lecky to be probably the ablest book ever published in defence of the reality of witchcraft.[5]

Casaubon, Hobbes, More, and Glanvill, each pointed out the emotional character of enthusiasm and offered a natural explanation of the phenomenon. In the last decade of the century, John Locke (1632-1704) incorporated, somewhat reluctantly, into his famous *Essay* a chapter on Enthusiasm as a ground of assent. Locke was attempting no speculative system of philosophy, but a more modest inquiry; he would know the things " which concern our conduct." [6] Man's mind is intended

to procure him the happiness which the world is capable of; which certainly is nothing else but plenty of all sorts of those things which can with ease, pleasure and variety, preserve him in it.[7]

[1] *Philosophia Pia,* pp. 89-90.

[2] *Ibid.,* p. 71.

[3] *Ibid.,* pp. 73-4.

[4] *Ibid.,* pp. 161-2. Glanvill also defines Reason as the innate ideas themselves. *Vide supra,* p. 68.

[5] Lecky, *op. cit.,* vol. i, p. 133.

[6] *Essay Concerning Human Understanding* (Oxford, 1894), bk. i, chap. i, 5.

[7] Peter, Lord King, *The Life of John Locke with extracts from his correspondence, Journal and Common-place Books* (London, 1829), p. 86, Journal, Feb. 8, 1677.

Locke's own ill health has been held to account for the further statement that man's knowledge is to enable him " to live in peace with his fellowmen, and this also he is capable of."[1] Thus with Locke knowledge was vitally connected with conduct; and both were involved in religion. That Locke's characteristic problem, how far man can attain certainty, was suggested by his religious interests has not always been remembered; although he himself said that it was a conversation with some friends on the " principles of morality and revealed religion " which started him on the studies that culminated in the famous *Essay*.[2]

Enthusiasm was especially distasteful to Locke, for it conflicted both with his conception of the ground of knowledge and with his desire to establish the reasonableness of religion. True, he had had very pleasant relations with at least one of the group whose principles he disliked. At Rotterdam Locke spent most of his two years' residence (1687-89) in the house of Benjamin Furly, one of George Fox's first converts.[3] With the gentle manner of the Quaker, Locke was much impressed. He seems even to have helped Furly in a controversy with a Baptist.[4] Toward the end of his life the great Englishman wrote to his former host:

> I live in fear of the bustlers, and would not have them come near me. Such quiet fellows as you are, that come without drum or trumpet, with whom we can talk upon equal terms, and receive some benefit by their company I should be glad to have in my neighborhood, or to see sometimes, though they came from the other side of the world.[5]

[1] King, *op. cit.*, p. 87.

[2] H. R. Fox Bourne, *The Life of John Locke* (London, 1876), vol. i, pp. 248-89.

[3] *Ibid.*, vol. ii, pp. 58 *et seq*.

[4] Thomas Forster, *Original Letters of Locke, Algernon Sidney and Anthony Lord Shaftesbury* (London, 1830), p. 17.

[5] Letter to Furly, October 12, 1702, quoted in Bourne, *op. cit.*, vol. ii, p. 506.

At Furly's Locke may well have seen a letter of the Quaker theologian, Robert Barclay, which Furly published in 1678. In this letter, which was part of a discussion that Barclay had with Herr Adrian Paets, once ambassador to Spain from the United Provinces, the doctrine of inner light was set forth in analogy to the doctrine of innate principles. Such a statement, if Locke had seen it, would have been doubly offensive in his eyes.[1]

The first three editions of the *Essay concerning Human Understanding* contained no notice of enthusiasm, but in 1695 Locke discussed with his friend, Sir Thomas Molyneux (1661-1733), possible additions to the *Essay*. Writing from Dublin under date of March 26, 1695, Molyneux expressed his opinion concerning the inclusion of a section on enthusiasm:

> I must freely confess, that if my notion of enthusiasm agrees

[1] Robert Barclay, *The Possibility & Necessity of the Inward and Immediate Revelation of the Spirit of God, Towards the Foundation and Ground of True Faith, Proved, In a Letter writ in Latin to the Herr Paets, And now also put into English*. . . . (London, 1703). Paets had made the usual distinction between necessary truths, that is, general principles such as, that God is; that a whole is greater than a part, etc., and contingent truths or matters of fact. The first class of truths, necessary truths, are innate in the mind; but the second class, contingent truths, are not innate and cannot be revealed directly to the mind. To this second class belongs the essence of Christianity, which consists in the knowledge of and faith concerning the birth, life, death, resurrection and ascension of Jesus. Therefore, the truths necessary to salvation cannot be innate in the mind or immediately revealed to the mind. Barclay denied that knowledge of the historical facts of Christ's life and work is the essential element of Christianity. These could be given immediately, but are not to be expected. But there are innate spiritual as well as natural ideas, and spiritual or supernatural senses by which these are perceived when they are stirred up by God working in us. Barclay's letter is also printed in William Sewel, *The History of the Rise, Increase and Progress of the Christian people called Quakers* (New York, 1844), vol. ii, pp. 231-243. This edition is reprinted from the second English edition of 1735.

with yours, there is no necessity of adding any thing concerning it, more than by the by, and in a single section in chap. 18, lib. iv. I conceive it to be no other than a religious sort of madness, and comprises not in it any more of thinking or operation of the mind, different from what you have treated of in your essay.[1]

Molyneux added that, if Locke cared to do so, he might treat of the absurdities which men embrace for religion. In his answer, Locke indicated that his conception of enthusiasm was much that of his friend. As for a history of religious absurdities, he could not attempt this, for it would be beside his purpose, and, moreover, space forbade it.

Why then did Locke include a chapter on enthusiasm in the fourth edition of his *Essay?* In answering such a question one must again recall Locke's religious interests. He was concerned to magnify natural religion, for only thus did he think to justify the reasonableness of faith. He readily admitted the possibility of revelation. " . . . I crave leave to say," he once wrote, " that he who comes with a message from God to be delivered to the world, cannot be refused belief if he vouches his mission by a miracle, because his credentials have a right to it." [2] Locke was aware that this admission opened the door to enthusiasm, as appears from an early entry in his *Journal*. On April 6, 1682, he wrote that he did not remember having heard of enthusiasm among the Americans (Indians) or among any " who have not pretended to a revealed religion." This suggested the thought which he did not conclude for lack of evidence:

Whether those that found their religion upon Revelation, do not from thence take occasion to imagine that since God has been pleased by Revelation to discover to them the general precepts of their religion; they that have a particular interest in

[1] Locke, *Works,* 11th edition (London, 1812), vol. ix, p. 353.
[2] *A Discourse of Miracles, Works,* vol. ix, p. 259.

his favour have reason to expect that he will reveal Himself to them . . . in those things that concern them in particular, in reference to their conduct, state or comfort.[1]

It is necessary, therefore, to distinguish enthusiasm from revelation.

In the fourth edition of the *Essay* appeared the chapter on Enthusiasm, its position indicating its relation to the general design. The Fourth Book, in which this new chapter occurs, is the real accomplishment of that which Locke set out to do—to consider the grounds of persuasion. Chapters xvii and xviii are concerned with reason and faith, chapter xix with enthusiasm.

Reason is defined as the discovery of the certainty or probability of such propositions or truths, which the mind arrives at by deduction made from such ideas, which it has got by the use of its natural faculties; viz. by sensation or reflection.[2]

Faith is the

assent to any proposition, not thus made out by the deductions of reason, but upon the credit of the proposer, as coming from God, in some extraordinary way of communication.[3]

Enthusiasm is

a third ground of assent, which with some men has the same authority, and is as confidently relied on as either faith or reason.[4]

To distinguish between faith and enthusiasm, both of which claim knowledge from God by extraordinary means, Locke analyzes the enthusiast's "idea." The enthusiast claims to see the inner light as clearly as one sees the sun

[1] King, *op. cit.*, p. 127.
[2] *Essay*, bk. iv, xviii, 2.
[3] *Ibid.*
[4] *Ibid.*, book iv, xix, 3.

and believes that one might as well take a glowworm to assist one in discovering the sun as to examine the celestial ray in the mind by the dim candle of reason.[1] But what does the enthusiast really perceive? When he professes to see the truth of a proposition or to feel an inclination to action, he doubtless tells the truth; but does the enthusiast at the same time perceive that the truth or the impulse comes from God? The idea perceived might be the work of spirits that are not of God; for there are spirits "which, without being divinely commissioned, may excite those ideas in me, and lay them in such order before my mind, that I may perceive their connexion."[2] To perceive that a proposition is true, or to feel an impulse to action, is one thing; to perceive that the proposition or the impulse is from God, is another thing. The latter can only be proven in the rational manner by which the historical truths of Christianity are demonstrated. Those who claim immediate inspiration are thus impaled upon the horns of a dilemma: they can not present rational proofs to substantiate the truth of that which they claim to receive immediately, for that which can be rationally demonstrated does not need a revelation to attest it; and, if they claim certainty merely on the basis of their own conviction, then, they are believing their illumination "to be a revelation only because they strongly believe it to be a revelation; which is a very unsafe ground to proceed on, either in our tenets or actions."[3]

Locke's contribution to the problem of enthusiasm is, then, his analysis of the consciousness of the enthusiast, and his attempted demonstration that enthusiasm rests upon a psychological and not a logical conviction.[4] But Locke did not

[1] *Essay,* book iv, xix, 8.
[2] *Ibid.,* book iv, xix, 10.
[3] *Ibid.,* book iv, xix, 11.
[4] George Sidney Brett, *A History of Psychology* (London and New

push his analysis to any satisfactory consideration of the grounds of psychological certainty. When one considers the treatises of Casaubon, More and Locke, it must be acknowledged that the earlier men are nearer modern psychology despite their antiquated science and forbidding terminology. Locke contributed much toward a sane estimate of enthusiasm, but he did little to explain the enthusiast.

It remained for a lesser man than Locke to see that conduct can not be based upon reason alone, and to suspect that enthusiasm might offer a clue to a more satisfactory ethical theory.

Shaftesbury's *Letter Concerning Enthusiasm* was evoked by the extravagances of the French prophets in London in 1708, concerning whose work he seems to have had some first-hand knowledge.[1] Other discussions of enthusiasm are scattered through his works, notably in *The Moralists, a Philosophical Rhapsody*, which was originally called *The Sociable Enthusiast; a Philosophical Adventure written to Palaemon*,[2] and in his *Miscellaneous Reflections*.

For his explanation of enthusiasm Shaftesbury falls back upon Cicero's suggestion, which Casaubon had already noticed in his treatise, that this state of mind takes its rise in the contemplation of something " prodigious and more than human:"

Something there will be of extravagance and fury, when the ideas or images received are too big for the narrow human vessel to contain. So that inspiration may justly be called

York, 1921), vol. ii, p. 351. This was, of course, not new: St. Thomas, for example, was fully aware of the difficulty. *Vide Summa,* secunda secundae, q. clxxi, art. 5.

[1] Benjamin Rand [ed.], *Life, Unpublished Letters and Philosophical Regimen of the Third Earl of Shaftesbury*. . . . (London, 1900), pp. xxvi, 336.

[2] *Letter Concerning Enthusiasm,* section 7.

divine Enthusiasm; for the word itself signified divine presence, and was made use of by the philosopher whom the earliest Christian fathers called divine, to express whatever was sublime in human passions.[1]

In his *Inquiry Concerning Virtue and Merit,* Shaftesbury set forth his ethical theory: nothing is " properly either goodness or illness in a creature, except what is from natural temper."[2] Goodness comes from the proper balancing or proportioning of the affections or passions, this balancing being done on a rational basis.[3] Such goodness, however, is not virtue or merit; these are possible only to rational creatures, who contemplating good and bad actions, form for the good an admiration which furnishes the basis for virtuous action.[4] This emotional admiration, which is paralleled by the admiration of beauty arising from the contemplation of proportion and harmony presented to the eye, is the real criterion of virtue. This Shaftesbury chose to call " enthusiasm," giving a new and respectable meaning to the despised word.

Reviewing the explanations of enthusiasm offered by the writers quoted in this chapter, one notes a consistent appeal to natural explanations and a minimum of that favorite resort of theologians, the charge of imposture. Moreover, the emotional origin of the enthusiast's certitude is generally recognized. If Locke missed this, he offered an analysis which had all the appearance of conclusiveness and which re-

[1] *Letter Concerning Enthusiasm,* section 7; *cf.* Casaubon, *Enthusiasme,* pp. 46-7.

[2] *Inquiry Concerning Virtue and Merit,* i, 2, 2. This was published first in 1699, but was reprinted in the *Characteristics* in 1711. The edition of the *Characteristics* used is that edited by John M. Robertson (London, 1900).

[3] Henry Sedgwick, *Outlines of the History of Ethics,* Fifth edition reprinted (London, 1910), p. 186.

[4] Shaftesbury, *Inquiry,* 1, 2, 3.

moved enthusiasm from the category of infallibility. A comparison of Casaubon's cautious language with Shaftesbury's supercilious manner is evidence of the completeness of this removal in the minds of philosophers. For the thinkers, at least, enthusiasm was now so little dangerous that the word itself could be borrowed for other uses.

CHAPTER V

Public Opinion of Enthusiasm

OTHER considerations than scholastic distinctions between *gratiae gratis datae* and *gratiae gratis facientes* or medical theories of the humours entered into the formation of public opinion concerning enthusiasm. Men who had to deal with enthusiasts in politics and business developed other than theoretical reasons for their distrust of those claiming an infallibility based upon immediate revelation. There were, too, certain changes in political, economic and religious conditions which made enthusiasm increasingly suspect. All these operated to enforce the arguments of pulpit and press and tended to lessen the popular disposition to believe in immediate inspiration. Lecky's statement concerning stories about witchcraft is equally true of enthusiasm. " Not until the predisposition was changed; . . . not until the sense of their improbability so overpowered the reverence for authority, as to make them disbelieve it even when they were unable to disprove it," [1] did men cease to treat seriously the assertion of the enthusiast that he had a direct message from the Almighty.

Not only in the writings of opponents but traditionally, enthusiasm was associated with madness. Benjamin Whichcote, the Cambridge Platonist, summed it up in one of his aphorisms: " Among Christians," he said, " those that pre-

[1] *History of the Rise and Influence of the Spirit of Rationalism*, vol. i, p. 103.

tend to be inspired seem to be mad; among the Turks, those that are mad are thought to be inspired."[1]

This traditional association of immediate inspiration with madness received corroboration from actual cases of insanity. An ordinance passed in 1650 provided punishments for any one not insane who should maintain any "meer creature" to be God.[2] There was much fanaticism bordering on insanity in the third quarter of the seventeenth century, some of it doubtless induced or aggravated by cruel punishments and deprivations, as under the Clarendon Code in the Restoration Period.[3]

Even when there was no actual insanity, the physical phenomena often attending the "visitation of the Spirit" helped to identify enthusiasm with madness. George Fox lost his sight as a result of pathological conditions, and once he lost both sight and hearing.[4] In the early eighteenth century, the French Prophets offer examples of these phenomena. An account of the Prophets records of a convert that,

when in his Bed, he fell into an extraordinary Fit of Agitation; in which Fit his Bed so shook upon the Floor, made such a Noise, that the People in other Rooms of the House thought a coach had gone up the Yard . . . .[5]

[1] Aphorism 1182, quoted by Tulloch, *Rational Theology and Christian Philosophy in England in the Seventeenth Century,* vol. ii, p. 112.

[2] The text of the Act was: "That all and every person and persons (not distempered with sickness, or distracted in brain) who shall presume avowedly in words to affirm and maintain him or her self, or any other meer Creature, to be very God. . . ." *Acts and Ordinances of the Interregnum* (London, 1911), vol. ii, p. 410.

[3] Note the epidemic of witch hunting that broke out in the half century following 1640 and the confessions often obtained under torture. *Vide* Notestein, *A History of Witchcraft in England from 1588-1718* (Washington, 1911), chaps. ix-xiv.

[4] *Journal,* 1648, p. 16; 1670, p. 267.

[5] Thomas Spinckes, *The New Pretenders to Prophecy Re-examined*

Sir Richard Bulkeley asserted, however, that in seizures the "inspired" did not change countenance, and that he had examined their pulse and found them "rather low, than high, and exactly (as near as one could judge) true and regular."[1]

The ecstatic character of enthusiastic preaching and praying was an additional factor in the association of abnormality with enthusiasm in popular opinion. Contemporaries were quick to note the effects of such preaching upon audiences, and to seek for explanations in natural terms. Dean Swift had his say about the matter: "Thus, it is frequent for a single vowel to draw sighs from a multitude; and for a whole assembly of saints to sob to the music of a solitary liquid."[2]

Other extravagant actions of enthusiasts, sometimes performed symbolically, caused contemporaries to suspect their sanity. A classic example in the ministry of George Fox is the Lichfield incident. After almost a year's imprisonment in Derby, Fox was walking with several Friends when he saw three church spires. Learning that these were in Lich-

(London, 1710), Appendix I, pp. 24-25. The following is a description of the enthusiastic fit of one of the Camisards in France in 1702. Denis Doustin, 28 years old, "aurait en un grand tremblement de toutes les parties de son corps, tenant la tête baissée marmottant entre ses dents: *é, oui, oui, filii, filia, meo,* ce qui'l aurait répété par plusieurs fois, comme s'il etait dans les convulsions. Et aurait continué ce tremblement, *miséricorde! grace! Seigneur!* battant des bras en répétant les memes mots." Charles Bast, "Les prophètes du Languedoc en 1701 et 1702" in *Revue Historique,* T. xxxvi, 270, p. 7 (1921).

[1] Sir Richard Bulkeley, *An Impartial Account of the Prophets* (London, 1707), p. 10. *Vide supra,* p. 57.

[2] Jonathan Swift, *A Discourse on the Mechanical Operation of the Spirit, Prose Works,* Temple Scott edition (London, 1908), vol. i, p. 203. Casaubon had already remarked concerning the preaching of his day, "that a man if he can utter any thing, which may seem to be extempore .... is by many .... deemed, I say, no lesse then inspired: this would make a man suspect, that as a decay of bodies is maintained in this elder age of the world; so probably, of wits must be granted." Casaubon, *A Treatise concerning Enthusiasme,* pp. 158-159.

field, Fox left the Friends and went across the fields toward the town, meeting some shepherds on the way. His *Journal* continues:

> I was commanded by the Lord, of a sudden, to untie my shoes and put them off. I stood still for it was winter, and the word of the Lord was like a fire in me, so I put off my shoes and was commanded to give them to the shepherds, and was to charge them to let no one have them except they paid for them. The poor shepherds trembled and were astonished.
>
> Then I walked on about a mile till I came into the town, and as soon as I was got within the town the word of the Lord came to me again, to cry, " Woe unto the bloody city of Lichfield! " So I went up and down the streets, crying with a loud voice, " Woe to the bloody city of Lichfield! " It being market-day, I went into the market-place, and to and fro in the several parts of it, and made stands, crying as before, " Woe to the bloody city of Lichfield! " And no one laid hands on me; but as I went thus crying through the streets, there seemed to me to be a channel of blood running down the streets, and the market-place appeared like a pool of blood.
>
> And so at last some Friends and friendly people came to me and said, " Alack, George, where are thy shoes? " I told them it was no matter.
>
> Now when I had declared what was upon me, and cleared myself, I came out of the town in peace; and returning to the shepherds, gave them some money, and took my shoes of them again.[1]

Fox attempted to explain his singular actions at Lichfield by reference to a tradition of wholesale martyrdom there in ancient times. He thought that his vision of blood might be accounted for as a vision of this slaughter. Unfortunately for Fox's theory, no such martyrdom occurred.

The supreme disregard of public opinion which character-

[1] *Journal,* 1651, pp. 39-40.

ized the Quakers led them to adopt bizarre methods of expressing their message, although many of their more extreme actions must be explained on pathological grounds. Some rejected clothes for a time; as Hume contemptuously put it: " A number of them fancied that the renovation of all things commenced, and that clothes were rejected together with other superfluities."[1] The term " Quaker " was a convenient handle for any unconventional religionist, and many things were probably laid at the door of the Quakers which belonged to other sects. At any rate, enthusiasm came to be associated with such spectacles as that which Pepys recorded in 1677:

> One thing extraordinary was, this day a man, a Quaker, came naked through the Hall Westminster only very civilly tied about the loins to avoid scandal, and with a chafing-dish of fire and brimstone burning about his head, did pass through the Hall, crying " Repent! Repent! "[2]

Owing to the *milieu* in which enthusiasm flourished as well as because of such controversies as that precipitated by Samuel How,[3] immediate inspiration was generally associated with the lower classes in society. The preaching of ignorant men was a major cause of reproach on the part of both Episcopalians and Presbyterians. Thomas Edwards, the heresiographer, complains " of all sorts of mechanicks, taking upon them to preach and baptize as smiths, taylors, shoomakers, pedlars, weavers, etc."[4] Another pamphleteer asks sarcastically: " Is it a miracle or wonder to see saucie

---

[1] David Hume, *The History of England* (New York, 1879), vol. v, p. 456. On the general subject, *vide* Braithwaite, *Beginnings of Quakerism*, p. 148 *et seq.*

[2] Wheatley's edition, vol. vii, p. 268.

[3] *Vide supra*, pp. 65-66.

[4] *Gangraena*, part ii, p. 29.

boys, bold botching taylors, and other most audacious, illiterate mechanicks to run out of their shops into a pulpit?"[1]

The sectaries of the seventeenth century were mainly from the lower classes. The Baptists, in 1614, declared that they were too poor to print their pamphlets; and in a petition to Charles II, in 1660, they stated that most of them earned their living by daily labor.[2] The more definitely enthusiastic sects proceeded from the same social stratum. Samuel Fisher (1608-1665), a Quaker controversialist, wrote: "the Quakers are mostly handicraftsmen."[3] During the period from 1650-1660, the Quakers were mainly from trading and yeoman classes, with some artisans and labourers, some merchants and a few gentry. The economic condition of the Quakers was bettered during the "second period," from 1660-1700, and some had grown wealthy.[4] Quaker historians usually attribute this change in economic status to the honesty and thrift of the Quakers; an Anglican writer remarks that mysticism could not remain attractive to the lower classes when the ferment of a revolutionary period had passed; while a socialist historian points out that, in the later period, laborers in the Quaker ranks were more cautious about admitting laborers to the fold while they brought up their own children for a higher type of work.[5] Later, the

---

[1] Quoted from *The Schismatics Sifted* (London, 1646), by Barclay, *Inner Life of the Religious Societies*, p. 157.

[2] Underhill [ed.], *Tracts on Liberty of Conscience and Persecutions, 1644-61*, pp. 72 and 299.

[3] Quoted in Thomas Hancock, *The Peculium; an endeavour to throw light on some of the causes of the Decline of the Society of Friends*. . . . (London, 1907), p. 124n.

[4] *Vide* Braithwaite, *Beginnings of Quakerism*, p. 312, and *Second Period of Quakerism*, pp. 460-462.

[5] *Ibid.;* Henry Melvill Gwatkin, *Church and State in England to the Death of Queen Anne* (London, 1917), p. 342; Eduard Bernstein, *Kommunistische und demokratisch-sozialistische Strömungen während der*

French Prophets also found adherents among the lower classes; some were servant maids, while many were ignorant. The adherence of gentlemen like John Lacy (fl. 1737) and Sir Richard Bulkeley, together with some others of an income of one to four thousand pounds yearly, called forth the outraged protests of several pamphleteers.[1]

Enthusiasm was not only connected with the lower classes in society, but was associated with dangerous political and social movements, a connection which goes back, of course, at least as far as the voluntary communism of the primitive Christian community in Jerusalem. The Levellers, who represented advanced democratic views, sometimes justified their political position by reference to immediate revelation. "The Levellers," wrote the Dean of Durham, in 1678, "do make out their Free-born Community with Arrows fitted from this Quiver."[2] Gerrard Winstanley (fl. 1648-1652), "the Digger," who held that "all mankind ought to have a quiet subsistence and freedom to live upon earth; and that there be no bondman nor beggar in all his holy mountain," and that all should have equal right to the ground, appealed to immediate inspiration as confidently as did George Fox:

englischen Revolution des 17. Jahrhunderts, in *Die Geschichte des Sozialismus in Einzeldarstellungen,* Erster Band, Zweiter Theil (Stuttgart, 1895), pp. 680 *et seq.*

[1] *Vide supra,* p. 56.

[2] Comber, *Christianity no Enthusiasm,* p. 90. Even men like Goodwin and Nye were accused of resting their case on immediate inspiration. There is a curious MS. note on the fly-leaves of a British Museum copy of Dr. Casaubon's edition of the astrologer John Dee's *A True & Faithful Relation of what passed for many Yeers between Dr. John Dee . . . . and Some Spirits* (London, 1659), which declares: "I remember well when this Booke was first publish'd that the then persons who Held the government had a Solemne Consult upon the suppressing it as looking upon it as publish'd by the Church of England men in reproach of them who then pretended so much to Inspiration: & Goodwyn Owen & Nye &c were great sticklers against it, but it was so quickly published & spread & so eagerly bought up as being a great & curious Novelty, that it was beyond theyr power to suppresse it."

I was made to appeal to the Father of Life, in the speaking of my heart likewise thus—Father, thou knowst that what I have writ or spoken concerning this light, that the Earth should be restored and become a Common Treasury for all mankind, without respect of persons, was thy free revelation to me. I never read it in any book, I heard it from no mouth of flesh, till I understood it from thy teaching first within me.[1]

Comber, in his book against the Quakers, called attention to the resemblance between Winstanley's doctrine and the teaching of the Quakers, and to the further facts, that the scenes of some of the Quakers' work were identical with those of the Leveller activities, and that the same printer, Giles Calvert, published tracts of both movements.[2] The fact that the Quakers refused to doff their hats in salutation to anyone got them into no end of trouble. Fox's refusal to lift his hat to the judges of the courts before which he was haled earned him especially hard treatment; and William Penn's insistence, when he was in the navy, upon wearing his hat in the presence of his admiral was a cause of much embarrassment to that worthy official. This denial of "worship" to human beings seemed to contemporaries to threaten the stability of all social institutions.

Some of the Ranters seem to have preached community of goods; and the Baptists, in their *Declaration* of 1647, thought worth while to vindicate their beliefs as to magistracy, "propriety" and polygamy.[3] The Fifth Monarchy

[1] For Gerrard Winstanley, *vide* Lewis H. Berens, *The Digger Movement in the Days of the Commonwealth.* . . . (London, 1906). This quotation is given by Berens, p. 121.

[2] Comber, *op. cit.,* pp. 6-7. Rufus M. Jones does not agree that Winstanley influenced Fox, *Studies in Mystical Religion,* pp. 494-5.

[3] On the Ranters, *vide* Barclay, *Inner Life of the Religious Societies,* p. 419; Baxter, *Works,* vol. iii, pp. 299-300. On the political activities of the Baptists, *vide* L. F. Brown, *The Political Activities of the Baptists and Fifth Monarchy Men* (London, 1912); *A Declaration by Congregational Societies in and about the City of London.* . . . (London, 1647).

Men, whose machinations caused so much uneasiness in the period of the Commonwealth and immediately afterward, were not, as a group, enthusiasts; they sought to establish only an extreme form of the Puritan government by the saints. The fanciful interpretation of Scripture by which they got their doctrine of the Fifth Monarchy had warrant in the writings of Puritan and older theologians; but the names of Fifth Monarchy Men and of enthusiastic groups were popularly coupled together. In the spring of 1656, to cite only one instance, it was reported that many meetings were being held by "Fifth Monarchmen, Quakers, etc., who though they differ in other things, agree in destroying magistracy and ministry."[1]

In the early eighteenth century, any democratic doctrine was liable to be branded as both levelling and enthusiastic by the extreme group who could not think of the Interregnum without a shudder. Bishop Atterbury (1662-1732), writing in 1710, thunders against the author of a pamphlet entitled *Vox Populi Vox Dei:*

... if we trace him throughout all his Pamphlet, we shall find him no other than a Leveller, and consequently an implacable Enemy to any thing above himself, which is the most dangerous of Enthusiastick Delusions, or rather a desperate Contrivance of the Needy to bring all things into Common, or under that Colour to thrust themselves into the Estates they have no Title to.[2]

People generally were not disposed to look for nice distinctions between sects which were all alike suspect, and so the "saints" of the Commonwealth, Levellers and enthusiasts were lumped together:

[1] Quoted by Brown, *op. cit.,* p. 102.
[2] *The Voice of the People No Voice of God* (London, 1710), p. 24.

A numerous Host of dreaming Saints succeed;
Of the true old enthusiastic breed:
'Gainst form and order they their power employ,
Nothing to build, and all things to destroy.[1]

That there were levelling tendencies in the teachings of the enthusiasts can not be denied. Over against the ecclesiastical distinctions between clergy and laity, the enthusiast set his doctrine of immediate inspiration, which might come to the lowest of men. The Calvinists, whether Puritan or Presbyterian, were great advocates of political liberty; but their doctrine of election and their emphasis upon a learned ministry were fundamentally aristocratic. The enthusiasts, on the other hand, when they theorized at all, insisted upon an inner light or a divine seed in all men, not in the elect alone, and upon an inner authority to preach which depended neither on human learning nor ordination. Such individualism was subject to no outward test, and contemporaries feared such an inner light because,

'Tis a dark lanthorn of the spirit,
Which none see by, but those that bear it.[2]

In a calmer day, Hume was to conclude that enthusiasm is less favorable to priestly power than sound reason or philosophy, and is a friend to civil liberty.[3]

Not less fatal to the reputation of the enthusiasts than their real or fancied connection with radical political and social movements was the popular identification of enthusiasm with the interests and designs of the Roman Catholics.

---

[1] Dryden, *Absalom and Achitophel*, ll. 529-532. Quotation is from Christie's edition of poetical works (London, 1921), p. 105.

[2] Samuel Butler, *Hudibras,* with annotations and preface by Zachary Gray (Cambridge, 1744), Canto. 1.

[3] "Of Superstition and Enthusiasm," *Essays and Treatises on Several Subjects* (London, 1822), vol. i, pp. 60-66.

Dissenters as well as Churchmen could see the shadow of Rome upon those who claimed immediate inspiration. Richard Baxter detected "a strange combination of the endeavours of the papists and the devil in most of these late heresies."[1] The whole frame of the design had "a papish aspect."[2] Of the Quakers he says:

> Many Franciscan Fryers and other Papists, have been proved to be disguised Speakers in their Assemblies, and to be among them; and it's like are the very Soul of all these horrible Delusions.[3]

To sensational writers, Ignatius Loyola was the horrible example of enthusiasm. By profuse citation, they sought to show that he and other Catholic saints had claimed immediate inspiration through dreams and visions.[4] From this it was an easy step to compare the infallibility of enthusiasm with the infallibility of Rome:

> That the enthusiasts challenge [i. e. claim] the same infallibility which the papal church does, but are more intolerable in their claim; for Popery places it only in one person, the pretended head of the Church, the pope; and enthusiasm claims it, as belonging to every Christian among them, every particular member of the church.[5]

Bishop Burnet thought that a claim to secret directions from God overthrew the fundamental principles of the Reformation:

> And, indeed, it is hard to determine whether the referring all

---

[1] Baxter, *Of the Unpardonable Sin against the Holy Ghost, Practical Works*, vol. ii, p. 349.

[2] *Ibid.*

[3] *Reliquiae Baxterianae.* . . . (London, 1696), p. 77.

[4] *Vide* Henry Wharton, *The Enthusiasm of the Church of Rome.*

[5] Robert South, *Sermons* (Oxford, 1842), vol. iii, p. 79.

Controversies of Religion to one infallible judge, or the giving up of Men to the Heats of their own Fancies, be the most dangerous Principle.[1]

Along with the influences which led the nation to fear and despise enthusiasm must be chronicled an increasing disbelief in modern supernatural experiences. Lecky noted the "great sceptical movement" which followed the Restoration, when the gayer classes " from mocking the solemn gait, the nasal twang, and the affected phraseology of the Puritans" naturally proceeded to ridicule their doctrines.[2] The historian of rationalism was thinking of the decline of belief in witchcraft, but it was easier to doubt enthusiasm than to question witchcraft. Puritans agreed with Churchmen and were soon to agree with deists that immediate inspiration did not exist in the seventeenth and eighteenth centuries, whether or not it existed in the first or third.

It is true that too much must not be made of this decline, since there are all too many proofs that Jessop is right: " The prophets are not improved off the face of the earth." [3] Prophecies were popular throughout the period under discussion; but there is some evidence that the appeal to natural explanations, coupled with the general unpopularity of enthusiasm among the classes interested in the stability of church and state, was creating a general scepticism. Meric Casaubon was aware of the tendency to smile " with some kind of compassion " at the mention of devils and spirits; [4] and Glanvill said that it was accounted wit to laugh at belief in witches.[5]

---

[1] Quoted by Evans, *History of Modern Enthusiasm,* pp. 36-7, from Burnet's sermon on January 30, 1680.

[2] Lecky, *op. cit.,* vol. i, p. 127.

[3] *The Coming of the Friars,* p. 344.

[4] *Of Credulity and Incredulity; in Things Divine and Spiritual.* . . . (London, 1670), p. 28.

[5] *Sadducismus Triumphatus,* p. 7.

While the effect of natural explanations of enthusiasm by writers like Hobbes, More and Locke upon popular thinking can not be measured with any degree of accuracy, there is reason to think that the polemics of the pulpit may have helped to create a wide-spread distrust of claims to extraordinary gifts of the Spirit. In some cases these pulpit appeals contributed to the popular association of enthusiasm with physical abnormalities. For example, in October, 1682, Richard Baxter preached at St. Giles, Cripplegate, where Samuel Annesley, John Wesley's grandfather, was once vicar, on " The Cure of Melancholy and Overmuch-Sorrows By Faith and Physick." This sermon, which was printed for Annesley's son-in-law, John Dunton, gave several pages to medical prescriptions for religious melancholy, including advice to avoid cheese and beef, to purge with " Sena in Whey " and to drink a concoction of " six sliced Pippens " boiled in three pints of whey.[1]

Perhaps an indication of increasing scepticism as to the divine origin of enthusiasm is to be found in the evident anxiety of the French Prophets in England to examine and defend their own physical symptoms. Reference has been made to Sir Richard Bulkeley's account of the Prophets' physical condition;[2] another illustration may be added from the pen of one of the chief figures among these enthusiasts of the early eighteenth century. In a statement prefixed to *The French Prophet's Declaration; or, An Account of the Preachings, Prophecies and Warnings of Elias Marion . . .*[3] there is a somewhat detailed account of the prophetic frenzy:

When the Spirit of God is about to seize me, I feel a great

[1] *A Continuation of Morning-Exercise Questions and Cases of Conscience, Practically Resolved by Sundry Ministers. . . .* (London, 1683), Sermon II. Samuel Annesley edited this volume.

[2] *Vide supra*, p. 100.

[3] Published 1707.

Heat in my Heart and the parts adjacent; which sometimes has a shivering of my whole Body, going before it: At other times I am seiz'd all at once, without having any such preceding Notice. As soon as I find my self seized my Eyes are instantly shut up, and the Spirit causes in me great Agitations of Body, making me to put forth great Sighs and Throbings which are cut short as if I were labouring for Breath. I have also frequently very hard Shocks, but yet all this is without Pain, and without hindering me of the freedom of thinking. I continue this about a quarter of an Hour, more or less, before I utter one Word. At last I feel that the Spirit forms in my Mouth the Words which he will have me to pronounce, which are almost always accompanied with some Agitations, or extraordinary Motions, or at least with a great Constraint. Sometimes it is so, that the first word that I am to speak next, is already formed in my own Idea; but I am very often ignorant how that very Word will end, which the Spirit has already begun.

The writer's interest in his own symptoms and his anxious apologetic betrays a fear that readers generally will not be sympathetic.

But whatever the effect of polemical writings upon the public, certainly the temper of the times as determined by political and social conditions was not favorable to enthusiasm. William and Mary, and following them, Anne, inherited grave problems. Suspicion as to the legality of William's title to the throne was followed by uneasiness as to a Protestant succession. Abroad, England entered into the struggle against France which was not to end until Waterloo; at home, there was the untried policy of partial toleration, which involved the question whether the nation should go ahead to complete religious liberty or should recall the measure of freedom already granted. The constitution of the Whig Revolution was a compromise between discordant elements which united only against the common dangers of absolutism and Roman Catholicism. It was an attempted balance of the conflicting interests of parliament and king, Church and State, Establishment and Dissent. To preserve this unstable governmental craft in the period after 1689, quiet waters were necessary; and governmental necessity was supplemented by demands of the interest powerful in the latter seventeenth and in the eighteenth centuries, namely, trade. Disputes within and without only endangered commerce and decreased profits.

Whig moderation in politics expressed the common desire for peace in Church and State. The age of Walpole (1721-1741) was a period in which tumult within the nation and war with other nations were avoided in the interests of the Hanoverian succession and of the increasingly important commercial classes.

The tendency toward moderation in politics was supplemented by the tendencies in philosophy and in the developing natural sciences. The trend of philosophy was toward doubting all that could not be rationally demonstrated; and growing knowledge was showing how unreliable were many of the old assumptions about the world. The "rationalism" of the eighteenth century was, on the whole, a distrust of man's ability to arrive at more than reasonable probability; to claim more was pride.[1] *Gulliver's Travels* is the reaction of a sensitive mind toward the excessive claims of human beings to knowledge and culture. Men had better follow the dictates of "common sense," the accepted opinions of society.

Literature reflected a similar modesty. Prose, useful for political and social discussions, prevailed over poetry; and practical interests influenced even poetry, which was much occupied with satire, a political weapon of no little impor-

[1] *Vide* Arthur O. Lovejoy, "'Pride' and Eighteenth Century Thought," in *Modern Language Notes*, vol. xxxvi, no. 1 (January, 1921), pp. 31-37. Pride was a common charge against enthusiasts.

tance. One does not need to acquiesce in the opinion, once very common among students of literature, that the Age of Pope was devoid of both originality and imagination, to recognize the fact that individuality was repressed in the interest of correct form. Poetry itself was mainly confined within the polished limits of the couplet, and correctness and elegance of expression were the aims of the essayists. This might be expected in a literature that concerned itself largely with the "town" and its doings, disdaining the country as crude and preferring the artificiality of formal gardens to the beauty of unspoiled landscapes.

The polite society of this period, like much of the literature that represents it, was occupied with correctness of form. The ceremonious formality of the age is too notorious to need illustration. Picturesque as that society seems now after two hundred years, it did not furnish literature with the inspiration needed. John Dennis complained that business and politics had so stamped men that there were not enough "originals," unique individuals, to furnish characters from which literary men might draw.[1]

Consonant with this temper of the early decades of the eighteenth century, desire for political peace, distrust of certainty in knowledge, a tendency toward correctness of form and the repression of originality in literature and in polite society, the ideal of religion was moderate piety. Religious dissension continued; but, compared with the previous century, sectarian feeling was, as Voltaire observed, "no more than the hollow noise of a sea, whose billows still heaved long after the storm."[2] The pious man subscribed to the demands of respectable society and carefully avoided the ex-

[1] John Dennis, *The Taste in Poetry*, reprinted in Durham, *Critical Essays of the Eighteenth Century* 1700-1725 (New Haven, 1916), pp. 138-139.

[2] Voltaire, *English Letters*, Letter V.

tremes of superstition and enthusiasm. The third Lord Shaftesbury, an example of the fine gentleman of the period as well as a philosopher, thanked God for a church

where zeal was not frenzy and enthusiasm; prayer and devotion not rage and fits of loose extravagance; religious discourses not cant and unintelligible nonsense; nor the character of a Saint resembling that of their inspired and godly men and women leaders; but where a good and virtuous life, with a hearty endeavour of service to one's country and mankind, joined with a religious performance of all sacred duties and a conformity with the established rites, was enough to answer the highest character of religion, and where all other pretenses to gifts or supernatural endowments beyond these moral and Christian perfections were justly suspected and treated as villainy, cheat, imposture, and madness.[1]

Matthew Green " of the Customhouse," in his poem, " The Spleen," summed up the position of many Churchmen of the period:

> But to avoid religious jars
> The laws are my expositors,
> Which in my doubting mind create
> Conformity to Church and State.[2]

In an age that praised moderation and discounted all fanaticism, the word, enthusiasm, began to be a general term of reproach for extreme conduct of many kinds. A brief summary of some of the uses of the word itself will indicate certain qualities which were ordinarily associated with a claim to immediate inspiration.

The Rebellion and the Commonwealth were looked back

---

[1] Excerpt from unpublished treatise on "Enthusiasm," given in the Fourth Earl of Shaftesbury's Life of his father, in Benjamin Rand, *Life, Unpublished Letters and Philosophical Regimen* . . . , p. xxvii.

[2] Robert Dodsley [ed.], *A Collection of Poems* (London, 1766), vol. i, pp. 153-7.

upon as the high-water mark of error in English history; consequently, anything which seemed to threaten the established order was naturally enough connected with those turbulent days. A Nonjuror, Charles Leslie (1650-1722), regarded enthusiasm as the "true ground of occasional conformity," the device by which nonconformists could hold office. To him, "a Whig is a state enthusiast, as a dissenter is an ecclesiastical; they will be tied to no rules of government but of their own framing. . . ."[1] On the other hand, Henry Sacheverell (1674-1724), whose Tory sermon in St. Paul's in 1709 created no little disturbance, was denounced as an enthusiast by the Whigs.[2] Whatever threatened established order was enthusiastic. Zeal, even for religion, fell under the ban; and Addison could define enthusiasm as "a kind of excess of devotion."[3]

Obtrusive display of religion or of religious emotion was naturally offensive to a period sensitive to correct form and elegance of behavior. "A person wants good breeding, or is a very great enthusiast, who talks so much about religion."[4] Lord Shaftesbury had set the fashion of smiling in a superior way at the extravagances of enthusiasts, and this method was carried out with a right good will by the playwrights and satirists: polite society learned to laugh at the ill-breeding of enthusiasts, instead of trembling at sup-

[1] *The Theological Works of the Reverend Mr. Charles Leslie* (Oxford, 1832), vol. vi, pp. 469-70. The 1832 edition is a reprint, somewhat enlarged, of the original collected edition of Leslie's theological works published in 2 volumes folio, London, 1721. Leslie was a controversialist who wrote copiously against the deists, the Quakers, the Muggletonians, etc., in the interest of Anglicanism as interpreted by the Nonjurors.

[2] William Bissett, *The Modern Fanatick*. . . . (London, 1710), pp. 1-2.

[3] *Spectator,* edited by George A. Aitken (London, 1898), no. 201, October 20, 1711.

[4] *A Lash at Enthusiasm* (1774), quoted by J. E. V. Crofts, "Enthusiasm" in *Eighteenth Century Literature, an Oxford Miscellany.*

posed plots of the "inspired" to cut the throats of disbelievers. On the stage, the "prophet" furnished material for comedy. Thomas D'Urfey's (1653-1723) chorus sang:

> Strange Miracles we ne'er unfold,
>   We scorn to understand 'em;
> Those shewn the Mob in Days of old
>   Provok'd, but did not mend 'em;
>   We cant in Tone,
>   We sigh, we groan,
>   Nor do our Gambols tire us;
>   And tho' our Preaching be Hum-drum,
>   And Writing senceless as Tom Thumb,
>   We still have Fools Admire us.[1]

Significant also of a change in public opinion is the fact that "enthusiasm" began to be used to express other and more harmless ideas than that of immediate inspiration, but ideas which yet had relation to the older meaning. Attention has already been called to the employment of the word by Shaftesbury in drafting his ethical theory.[2] In 1704 John Dennis had used the word in elaborating his grounds of criticism. The greater poetry, he held, "is an Art by which a Poet justly and reasonably excites great Passion. . . ."[3] There are two kinds of passion: vulgar and enthusiastic. The latter is "Passion which is moved by the Ideas in Contemplation, or the Meditation of things that belong not to common Life."[4]

This is not the place for a discussion of the relation of en-

[1] Thomas D'Urfey, *The Modern Prophets*... (London, 1709—Lowndes date).

[2] *Vide supra*, p. 96.

[3] John Dennis, *The Grounds of Criticism in Poetry* (1704), reprinted in Durham, *Critical Essays of the Eighteenth Century*, p. 150.

[4] *Ibid.*, p. 151.

thusiasm to the Romantic Movement in literature, but the use of the word for states of mind similar to those of the enthusiast, in the stricter sense, is an indication of the passing of the older attitude toward immediate inspiration.[1]

The poem of Joseph Warton (1722-1800), which, according to Courthope, is the first deliberate expression in England of the feeling out of which grew the Romantic Movement in literature, is called " The Enthusiast." In this poem, the name is justified in that the enthusiast loses himself in the contemplation of Nature, a forecast of the mystical attitude toward Nature which was to play such an important part in the later Romantic Movement.

> But never let me fail in cloudless nights,
> When silent Cynthia in her silver car
> Through the blue concave slides, when shine the hills,
> Twinkle the streams, and woods look tip'd with gold,
> To seek some level mead, and there invoke
> Old Midnight's sister, Contemplation sage,
> (Queen of the rugged brow and stern-fixt eye)
> To lift up soul above this little Earth,
> This folly-fetter'd world; to purge my ears,
> That I may hear the rolling planet's song,
> And tuneful turning spheres.[2]

William Whitehead (1715-1785), in his poem of the same name, makes this contemplation of Nature a step toward God:

> Here Contemplation points the road
> Through Nature's charms to Nature's God;
> These, These, are joys alone.[3]

---

[1] The relation of enthusiasm to Romanticism is being studied by Miss M. D. Long, of Sweet Briar College.

[2] Alexander Chalmers [ed.], *The Works of the English Poets*, vol. xviii, pp. 160-1. On Warton, *vide* Courthope, *History of English Poetry* (London, 1919), vol. v, p. 379.

[3] Chalmers, *op. cit.*, vol. xvii, p. 319.

The enthusiast of this early Romantic poetry was one who withdrew within, disdaining the conventions of his fellows; he "wandered lonely as a cloud," seeking solitary communion with Nature. Whitehead's enthusiast is rebuked for his desertion of society:

> I stop, I gaze; in accents rude
> To thee, serenest Solitude,
>   Bursts forth th' unbidden lay;
> Begone, vile world; the learn'd, the wise,
> The great, the busy, I despise;
>   And pity ev'n the gay.

Then Reason whispers in his ear:

> What mean'st thou, man? would'st thou unbind
> The ties which constitute thy kind,
>   The pleasures and the pains?
> Art thou not man? and dar'st thou find
> A bliss which leans not to mankind?
>   Presumptuous thought, and vain!
> Each bliss unshar'd is unenjoy'd,
> Each power is weak, unless employ'd
> Some social good to gain.
>
> Enthusiast, go; try every sense:
> If not thy bliss, thy excellence,
>   Thou yet hast learn'd to scan.
> At least thy wants, thy weakness know;
> And see them all uniting show
>   That man was made for man.[1]

In the light of the preceding discussion of the factors that influenced public opinion of enthusiasm, and of the public attitude resulting therefrom in the early part of the eighteenth century, the state of public opinion on enthusiasm in

---

[1] Chalmers, *op. cit.*, vol. xvii, pp. 219-20.

the period that saw the rise of the Methodist Movement may be summarized as follows:

Enthusiasm, immediate communion with God or a claim thereto, was regarded as akin to madness; or it was feared as somehow connected with dangerous political and social theories and movements. It was further associated in the minds of the people with the lower classes in whose interests the " glorious Revolution " had not been undertaken and who were to wait another century for the beginnings of political recognition. So great was the demand for civil tranquility, in the period succeeding the accession of William and Mary, that excessive zeal in religion and even violation of accepted standards of taste and conduct came to be looked upon as partaking of the dangerous nature of enthusiasm.

In the meanwhile, there are evidences that a new intellectual climate was being slowly created, and the old fear of immediate inspiration was being dulled by a wide-spread scepticism as to its possibility. Not least among these evidences is the employment against enthusiasm of ridicule instead of persecution, and the championing of emotion as the basis of ethical conduct and aesthetic appreciation. At least partially released from a haunting fear of reality in the enthusiast's claims, men were beginning to turn the very word to respectable uses.

CHAPTER VI

METHODIST ENTHUSIASM

The present study ends with a brief survey of Methodism: the reasons for the accusations of enthusiasm brought against the movement; the belief of the founder, John Wesley; and the place of Methodism in the history of enthusiasm.

The Methodist movement is ordinarily said to have begun in 1729 at Oxford with the " Holy Club ", a group of young men who at that time, under the leadership of John Wesley, were associated for the purpose of more diligent study, the cultivation of personal piety and the performance of charitable works. While this group at Oxford gained for themselves the name of " Methodists " and were the ones among whom developed the leadership of the evangelical movement called by that name, the true Methodist revival did not begin until after the " conversion " of John Wesley in Aldersgate Street in 1738, which marked for him the beginning of a religious experience epochal for his later preaching. The characteristics of the Oxford group, however, persisted in large measure in the movement to which it led; and the attacks made upon the Oxford Methodists were repeated in later years when the emphasis of the movement had changed from personal piety and charitable work as a means to religious peace, to religious experience resulting in piety and good works. These attacks show how much at variance with accepted standards of religion were the practices and principles of the Oxford group, and how persistent was the strain of pietistic zeal in later Methodism.

The first printed attack on the Methodists appeared in *Fogg's Weekly Journal,* December 9, 1732. The letter doubtless gives a fair picture of the impression which the Oxford group made upon many of their contemporaries:

These Methodists pretend to great refinements, as well as to what regards the speculative, as the practical part of religion; and have a very near affinity to the Essenes among the Jews, and the Pietists in Switzerland. The chief hinge, on which their whole scheme of religion turns, is, that no action whatever is indifferent; and hence they condemn several actions as bad, which are not only allowed to be innocent, but laudable, by the rest of mankind. They avoid, as much as possible, every object that may affect them with any pleasant or grateful sensations. All social entertainments and diversion are disapproved of; and, in endeavouring to avoid luxury, they not only exclude what is convenient, but what is absolutely necessary for the support of life; fancying (as is thought), that religion was designed to contradict nature. They neglect and voluntarily afflict their bodies, and practice several rigorous and superstitious customs, which God never required of them. All Wednesdays and Fridays are strictly to be kept as fasts; and blood let once a fortnight, to keep down the carnal man. At dinner, they sigh for the time they are obliged to spend in eating. Every morning to rise at four o'clock, is supposed a duty; and to employ two hours a day in singing of psalms and hymns, is judged an indispensable requisite to the being a Christian. In short, they practice everything contrary to the judgment of other persons, and allow none to have any (religion) but those of their own sect, which is the farthest from it.[1]

The way of life chosen by the Oxford Methodists was popularly ascribed, according to the author of the above, to various causes: to lack of money, to hypocrisy, or to superstition, enthusiasm and madness.

[1] Luke Tyerman, *The Life and Times of the Rev. John Wesley, M.A., Founder of the Methodists* (New York, 1872), vol. i, p. 85.

Wesley denied the charge of excessive fasting;[1] but a rigoristic tendency marked his teaching and practice. He grew in tolerance in his later years, but he always made much of the line of demarcation which separates true Christians from the world:

Here is a short, a plain, an infallible rule, before you enter into particulars. In whatever profession you are engaged, you must be singular, or be damned! The way to hell has nothing singular in it; but the way to heaven is singularity all over. If you move but one step towards God, you are not as other men are.[2]

Bishop Lavington,[3] one of the most determined of Wesley's opponents, cites the condemnation of rich clothes and furniture, and of recreations such as card-playing, dancing and theater-going as an instance of Methodist enthusiasm. There is need of redress in these matters, thinks the Bishop; but " Moderation, Reason and Scripture are Things unregarded by Enthusiasts, who must act in character."[4] While the French Prophets had been condemned for their laughing fits, the Methodists were accused of not laughing at all,[5] an accusation which is hardly accurate so far as the Wes-

[1] Letter to Richard Morgan of Dublin, October 18, 1732, printed in *The Journal of the Rev. John Wesley, A.M.,* . . . Standard Edition, Edited by Rev. Nehemiah Curnock (New York and Cincinnati, 1909-16), vol. i, p. 88. This edition is well-edited and indispensable to students of Methodism.

[2] Sermon xxvi, "Upon our Lord's Sermon on the Mount, Discourse xi," iii, 4 in Wesley's *Standard Sermons*, Edited and Annotated by Edward H. Sugden (London, 1921), vol. i, p. 541.

[3] George Lavington (1683-1762), bishop of Exeter, author of *The Enthusiasm of Methodists and Papists compar'd,* in three parts (London, 1749-51).

[4] Lavington, *op. cit.,* part i, pp. 20-24.

[5] *Ibid.,* part i, p. 20.

leys were concerned, but which was certainly not altogether without foundation. The "grave-yard" poets, such as Blair, Young and Thomson, were always popular with the Methodists, and a minor note appears in much of Charles Wesley's verse.[1]

The rigorousness of the Methodist piety was rendered more odious to eighteenth-century eyes by the missionary zeal of Methodist preachers. John and Charles Wesley went to Georgia with General Oglethorpe in 1735, the former going as a missionary to the Indians, the latter as secretary to Oglethorpe. Bishop Lavington records as a trait very common among enthusiasts " a restless impatience and insatiable thirst of Travelling, and undertaking dangerous Voyages, for the Conversion of Infidels; together with a declar'd Contempt for all dangers, pains, and Sufferings." And further on he speaks of " the natural unsettled humour, the rapid motion of Enthusiastic heads." [2]

The expedition to America, undertaken, as Wesley says, to save the souls of the missionaries themselves, was not so offensive as the conduct of the brothers after their return to England. This is not the place to enter into either a detailed

---

[1] " The last time I had the honour of hearing a sermon by Mr. Benson, one of their most popular preachers, I could not help remarking that Thomson, Young, Blair, and Charles Wesley, contributed as much, or more, to that discourse, as the writers of the four gospels, or even St. Paul himself. It is true, Mr. Benson spouted well, and his favourite authors were introduced with spirit and grace. I must, however, be allowed to conjecture, that when Thomson wrote 'The Seasons', Young 'The Night Thoughts', and Blair 'The Grave', none of them dreamed, poets as they were, that they were at that time composing Methodist sermons." Joseph Nightingale, *A Portraiture of Methodism* (London, 1807), p. 256. In 1745, John Wesley paid to Robert Dodsley, the publisher, £50 as damages for printing a considerable part of Young's *Night Thoughts* without authority. John Wesley's *Journal,* vol. iii, p. 162n.

[2] Lavington, *op. cit.,* part i, p. 26.

account of the progress of Methodism or of the theological questions involved; but the present interest will be served by calling attention to the fact that in the month of May, 1738, John Wesley had an experience in a religious society which met in a house in Aldersgate Street, London, "where one was reading Luther's preface to the *Epistle to the Romans.*" That experience Wesley describes by saying:

. . . I felt my heart strangely warmed. I felt I had trust in Christ, Christ alone for salvation; and an assurance was given me that He had taken away *my* sins, even *mine*, and saved *me* from the law of sin and death.[1]

If the Methodists had broken over the bonds of convention before, they transgressed fourfold after they gained a confidence born of such experiences. Prevented from preaching in many of the churches, partly because of attacks upon the lives and methods of the clergy, the Wesleys and their friends began the itinerating missionary ministry which was henceforth to characterize their work. The manner of their preaching soon awoke intense opposition.

The Rev. Theophilus Evans in his *The History of Modern Enthusiasm, from the Reformation to the Present Times,* thus describes the exhortations of the Methodists:

The Manner of the Itinerants' holding-forth is generally very boisterous and shocking, and adapted, to the best of their Skill, to alarm the Imagination, and to raise a Ferment in the Passions, often attended with screaming and trembling of the Body. The Preacher now grows more temptestuous and dreadful in his Manner of Address, stamps and shrieks, and endeavours all he can to increase the rising Consternation, which is sometimes spread over a great Part of the Assembly in a few Minutes from its first Appearance. And to compleat the Work, the Preacher has his Recourse still to more frightful Representations; that

[1] *Journal,* May 24, 1738, vol. i, p. 475.

he sees Hell-flames flashing in their Faces; and that they are *now! now! now! dropping into Hell! into the Bottom of Hell! the Bottom of Hell!*[1]

The account is untrue to the general standard of John Wesley, but even his preaching sometimes exceeded what was considered the bounds of good taste. Horace Walpole once heard Wesley and conceded that there were parts and eloquence in it, but added: " Towards the end he exalted his voice, and acted very ugly enthusiasm."[2]

Along with emotional sermons, Methodist singing appeared enthusiastic. In a " Picture " of Methodist enthusiasm, their music is described as follows:

And, as to their Singing, they, perhaps, have got some of the most melodious Tunes that ever were composed for Church Music; there is great Harmony in their Singing, and it is very inchanting. I say very inchanting; because the Hymns they Sing, i. e. all I have seen or heard of, are not rational Compositions, nor do they accord with the first Principles of all Religion, but like their Prayers, dwell upon a Word, or are immediate addresses to the Son of God, as the supreme Object of Worship. And do represent him as much more friendly and compassionate to the human World than God the Father ever was—so that their Singing is calculated to engage the Passions by nothing more than Words, and the Melody of the Sound, or Voice; but if you would sing with the Understanding, you must have other sorts of Compositions both for Psalmody and Prayer, than what the Foundery or the Tabernacle do afford you.[3]

The effects of such preaching and singing were often

[1] Evans, *op. cit.,* p. 119. The quotation is from the second edition (London, 1757).

[2] *Letters* (Cunningham's edition), vol. v, p. 16.

[3] John Scott, *A Fine Picture of Enthusiasm* (London, 1744), p. 24. The " Foundery " and the " Tabernacle " were the London headquarters of Wesley and Whitefield respectively.

startling enough, especially at the beginning of the movement. In June, 1739, John Wesley recorded:

> While I was earnestly inviting all sinners to " enter into the holiest " by this " new and living way " many of those that heard began to call upon God with strong cries and tears. Some sunk down, and there remained no strength in them; others exceedingly trembled and quaked; some were torn with a kind of convulsive motion in every part of their bodies, and that so violently that often four or five persons could not hold one of them. I have seen many hysterical and many epileptic fits; but none of them were like these in many respects. I immediately prayed that God would not suffer those who were weak to be offended. But one woman was offended greatly, being sure they might help it if they would—no one should persuade her to the contrary; and was got three or four yards when she also dropped down, in as violent an agony as the rest. Twenty-six of those who had been thus affected (most of whom, during the prayers which were made for them, were in a moment filled with peace and joy) promised to call upon me the next day. But only eighteen came; by talking closely with whom I found reason to believe that some of them had gone home to their house justified. The rest seemed to be waiting patiently for it.[1]

The whole quotation has been given, for the student of Methodism must remember that contemporaries formed their opinions of the movement not only from observing such scenes as this one, but more especially from reading such accounts as the above, which contains both a description of the occurrence and Wesley's interpretation of it. An even more graphic description occurs in a letter from a helper, John Cennick:

> On Monday night, I was preaching at the school, on the forgiveness of sins, when numbers cried out with a loud and bitter cry. Indeed, it seemed that the devil and the powers of dark-

[1] John Wesley, *Journal*, vol. ii, p. 221-222.

ness were come among us. My mouth was stopped. The cries were terrifying. It was pitch dark; it rained much; and the wind blew vehemently. Large flashes of lightning and loud claps of thunder mingled with the screams and exclamations of the people. The hurry and confusion cannot be expressed. The whole place seemed to resemble the habitation of apostate spirits; many raving up and down, and crying " The devil will have me; . . . I am gone, gone for ever!" . . . Some cried out with a hollow voice, " Mr. Cennick! Bring Mr. Cennick!" I came to all that desired me. Then they spurned me with all their strength, grinding their teeth, and expressing all the fury that heart can conceive. Their eyes were staring and their faces swollen, and several have since told me, that when I drew near, they felt fresh rage, and longed to tear me in pieces. I never saw the like, not even the shadow of it before. Yet I was not in the least afraid, as I knew God was on our side.[1]

If Bishop Warburton had heard of this scene, he must have considered that he had used moderation in his statement that the new birth " began in storms and tempests, in cries and ecstasies, in tumult and confusion.[2]

The connection of the lower social classes with the enthusiastic sects of the preceding century helped, as has been shown, to determine the public attitude toward enthusiasm; and there is evidence that Methodists evoked a similar association of ideas. Evans says of the Methodists: " It is in fact the Revival of the Enormities and Licentiousness of the last Age, now above a Century ago, when it was free for any silly Mechanick and illiterate Pretender to vent his Non-

[1] Quoted from a letter of Cennick to Wesley under date of September 12, 1739, by Tyerman, *The Life and Times of John Wesley,* vol. i, p. 263. Large quotations regarding such scenes are given by Tyerman, pp. 255-263.

[2] William Warburton, *The Doctrine of Grace; or the Office and Operations of the Holy Spirit Vindicated from the insults of infidelity and the Abuses of Fanaticism* . . . , p. 126. Such scenes as the above practically ceased after 1739. *Vide* Tyerman, *op. cit.,* vol. i, p. 263.

sense, not only with Impunity, but with Applause and Reverence."[1] The application of this remark is evident, since Wesley found it necessary to avail himself of the assistance of lay helpers who became itinerant preachers under Wesley's supervision. Of the thirty-five helpers whose autobiographies are included in the volumes entitled *Wesley's Veterans*,[2] twenty-three represent the following occupations which they or their fathers followed: miner, clothier, farmer soldier,[3] carpenter, mason, apprentice in worsted trade, tanner, gardener, cutler, apprentice in china trade and laborer. The father of one of the remainder was manager of a woolen factory; one of the preachers was a bookseller; one was a schoolmaster; one a builder; and one secretary to a justice of the peace. The other seven preachers did not think it worth while to make statements as to their mundane occupations. Wesley himself preferred to preach to the poor,[4] and to spend practically all of his time in the centers of population or in travelling to and from these centers. Students of his life have remarked that Wesley's preaching tours followed the line of England's industrial developments, within the territory marked off by London, Bristol and Newcastle-on-Tyne.[5]

Supporting this inference from the social classes from which Methodism was recruited was the evangelical doctrine of the equality of all men in the sight of God, particularly

[1] Evans, *The History of Modern Enthusiasm*, p. 122.

[2] This series of autobiographies was first published in Wesley's *Arminian Magazine* and was reprinted as *Early Methodist Preachers* (1837-8). They have been republished in part as *Wesley's Veterans: Lives of Early Methodist Preachers Told by Themselves*, edited by John Telford (London, 1914), 7 vols.

[3] More than a fourth of the lives in the *Early Methodist Preachers* were those of ex-soldiers, *Wesley's Veterans*, vol. i, p. 7.

[4] John Wesley, *Journal*, Nov. 17, 1759, vol. iv, p. 358.

[5] W. H. Fitchett, *Wesley and His Century* (Nashville, n.d.), p. 187.

as it expressed itself in the Arminianism of the Wesleys. This had a levelling tone highly offensive to a society organized on the principle of "superiority." A well-known comment of the Duchess of Buckingham, natural daughter of James II, illustrates this feeling. In writing to the Countess of Huntingdon, patroness of Whitefield, the Duchess said:

> I thank your ladyship for the information concerning the Methodist preachers. Their doctrines are most repulsive, and strongly tinctured with impertinence and disrespect toward their superiors, in perpetually endeavouring to level all ranks, and do away with all distinctions. It is monstrous to be told that you have a heart as sinful as the common wretches that crawl on the earth. This is highly offensive and insulting; and I cannot but wonder that your ladyship should relish any sentiments so much at variance with high rank and good breeding.[1]

The popular attitude toward the Methodists was both influenced and expressed by the often reiterated charge that the Methodists were allied with the Roman Catholics, the "Papists." Wesley's High Churchmanship during his early period, especially during his American sojourn, caused him to take such an attitude as was readily interpreted as "popery." In a book called *A True and Historical Narrative of the State of Georgia, published by the principal land-holders of that colony, so far as it relates to the conduct of Mr. John Wesley, during his residence there,* several reasons are given for regarding Wesley as a Roman Catholic. Wesley had been over-strict with Dissenters, while some suspected to be Roman Catholics had been "received and caressed by him as his First-rate Saints." Wesley's insistence upon a strict observance of the canons and the introduction of certain practices, such as mixing wine with water in the Sacrament of

---

[1] Tyerman, *The Life of the Rev. George Whitefield*, Second Edition (London, 1890), vol. i, pp. 160-161.

the Lord's Supper, aroused suspicion and hostility, as did also his strict discipline.[1] But the accusations continued long after the founder of Methodism had passed out of this period of his life. Wesley records his astonishment in picking up Archdeacon Blackburne's *Considerations on the Penal Laws against Papists*[2] and finding therein this statement, " said to be wrote by a gentleman at Paris ":

> The Popish party boast much of the increase of the Methodists, and talk of that sect with rapture. How far the Methodists and Papists stand connected in principles I know not; but I believe it is beyond a doubt that they are in constant correspondence with each other.[3]

The Archdeacon noted to this letter, " I would willingly hope some doubt may be made of this."[4] There are numerous references in the *Journal* to this charge of popery, and, in 1744, when the country was excited over the threatened invasion of the Pretender and a proclamation had been issued (February 25th) commanding all Papists to leave London and Westminster, Wesley composed an address to the King, denying that Methodists were Papists and protesting their loyalty. On the advice of his brother, Charles, however, the address was laid aside.[5] The most elaborate presentation of the supposed connection between the Methodists and Roman Catholics was in the well-known work of Bishop Lavington, *The Enthusiasm of Methodists and Papists Com-*

---

[1] Given, in part, in *Journal,* vol. viii, p. 304, Appendix xviii.

[2] Francis Blackburne, Archdeacon of Cleveland, *Considerations on the Present State of the Controversy between the Protestants and Papists of Great Britain and Ireland; particularly on the Question, How far the Latter are entitled to a Toleration upon Protestant Principles* (London, 1768).

[3] *Journal,* vol. v, p. 295.

[4] *Ibid.,* p. 296.

[5] *Ibid.,* vol. iii, pp. 123-4.

par'd, which was published in three parts, 1749-51. Lavington sought to show that the Methodists were guilty of the same conduct and pretences as were found in the Roman Catholic Church, and he compared the Methodists with such saints as Francis, Dominic, Ignatius Loyola, Anthony of Padua and Catherine of Siena. Both Methodists and Papists commonly begin their work with field preaching.[1] Both abuse the clergy,[2] put on a sanctified appearance,[3] and teach sudden conversion, assurance of salvation and perfection.[4] The chief " comparison " is in the pretence of inspiration:

> Here we have the true Spirit, and very Essence of Enthusiasm, that ungrounded pretence to Inspiration; which of course makes men peremptory and pertinacious, sets them above carnal reasonings, and all conviction of plain Scripture; and obligeth them upon their own Principles to assume an Infallibility.[5]

In Lavington's words there recurs the old fear of enthusiastic infallibility; the controversy is again on familiar ground. Edmund Gibson (1669-1748), Bishop of London, outlined the objections of moderate churchmen in terms which reflected the position taken by his predecessors in the previous century. Gibson held " the firm conviction that nothing could prevent a recurrence of the disorders of the Commonwealth, aggravated by the anarchic influences of infidel speculations, save the maintenance of the national Church in all its privileges."[6] Consequently, he looked with great suspicion upon some aspects of Methodism, and,

---

[1] Lavington, *op. cit.,* part i, p. 11.
[2] *Ibid.,* part i, pp. 11-15.
[3] *Ibid.,* part i, pp. 18-19.
[4] *Ibid.,* part i, pp. 40-48.
[5] *Ibid.,* part i, p. 49.
[6] Norman Sykes, *Edmund Gibson Bishop of London.* . . . (Oxford and London, 1926), p. 284.

while personally kind to the Wesleys, he warned his diocese against their " enthusiasm " in no uncertain terms.

Writing a pastoral letter in 1739, Gibson declared that enthusiasm comes from a failure to distinguish rightly between ordinary and extraordinary gifts of the Holy Spirit. The latter have long since ceased, and only ordinary gifts, and these confined to their fruits and effects in the lives of Christians, remain in the church of this day.[1] The bishop proceeded to list a number of instances, copiously illustrated from Whitefield's Journals, for which he demanded " Evidences of a divine Commission." The list includes a claim of extraordinary communications from God and " more than ordinary Assurances of a special Presence with them; " language implying " a special and immediate Mission from God; " a profession of divine inspiration in thought and act; a claim to divine power in preaching and its effects; attempt at prophecy; representation of a new gospel " unknown to the Generality of Ministers and People, in a Christian Country." [2]

Methodist claims to " extraordinary communications " and to more than ordinary assurance of divine presence appeared particularly in their doctrines of conversion and of the witness of the Spirit. In regard to the first, Gibson takes a sympathetic view, but objects strenuously to certain aspects of the Methodist interpretation:

> But I hope, when your Ministers preach to you the Doctrine of Regeneration or being born again of the Spirit, as laid down in the New Testament; they do not tell you that it must be instantaneous, and inwardly felt at the very Time; both, because there is no such thing revealed to us by Christ or his Apostles,

[1] *The Bishop of London's Pastoral Letter to the People of his Diocese; . . . . By way of Caution, Against Lukewarmness on one hand and Enthusiasm on the other.* The Second Edition (London, 1739), pp. 19-20.
[2] *Ibid.*, pp. 27-37.

who lay down the Doctrine in general Terms; and because Experience shews us, that the Renovation of the Heart and Life is effected by Degrees, and discovers itself more and more, in a Hatred of Sin, and in a gradual Progress and Improvement in those Graces, which the Scripture declares to be the Fruits of the Spirit.[1]

In a similar spirit Gibson advised his clergy to teach men to judge their spiritual condition " from the Present Dispositions of their Hearts, and the Tenour of their lives, and the Improvements they make in Grace and Goodness; and not from any sudden and extraordinary influences and impulses." [2] The Bishop of Lichfield and Coventry, in a charge to his clergy, considers this claim to a "testimony of the Spirit" as a present privilege of Christians as a misapplication by enthusiasts of a passage of Scripture which belongs exclusively to primitive Christianity.[3]

[1] *Bishop of London's Letter*, pp. 45-46.
[2] *Ibid.*, p. 46.
[3] Quoted, *A Farther Appeal to Men of Reason and Religion*, part i, v, 8-9. *The Works of the Rev. John Wesley* (London, 1872), vol. viii, pp. 83-85. The orthodox Catholic doctrine was that a Christian does not ordinarily have assurance that he is saved. According to Thomas Aquinas, a Christian may know that he has grace by revelation, *ex speciali privilegio*..., or by a deduction from the fact that he hates the world and delights in God, etc. (*Summa,* prima secundae, quaestio cxii, articulus v). This interpretation was confirmed by the action of the Council of Trent, which declared that none can know with certainty whom God hath elected except by special revelation, *nisi ex speciali revelatione* ("Decretum de Justificatione," cap. xii, Schaff, *The Creeds of Christendom,* vol. ii, p. 103). To take any other stand would have betrayed the doctrine of the Church that grace is mediated through the sacraments; to know of a certainty that one is saved is to realize that one is beyond need of the Church's ministration. The Reformers recognized assurance as possible: but Luther's position, clear at first, was not set forth definitely in his later years owing to his fear of the enthusiasts; and Calvin held that assurance, though possible, is not always attained without difficulty and uncertainty. Thus the Westminster Confession in chapter xviii, *De certitudine gratiae et salutis* (Schaff, *op. cit.,* vol. iii, p. 638), declares

In addition to conversion and the "witness of the Spirit," the Methodists talked of the Spirit dwelling in the believer in a manner that shocked their contemporaries. Indeed, the conduct of the Methodists was sometimes such as to give credit to the charge that they thought themselves inspired in what the theologians of the day called an "extraordinary manner." Isaac Watts (1674-1748), famous Nonconformist divine and hymn-writer, in a letter dated August 15, 1739, wrote of Whitefield as follows:

I wish Mr. Whitefield would not have risen above any pretences to the ordinary influences of the Holy Spirit, unless he could have given some better evidences of it. He has acknowledged to me in conversation that he knows an impression on his mind to be divine, though he cannot give me any convincing proofs of it.[1]

The Methodists were charged further with assuming that they were under the special care of God, who worked miracles in their favor. For example, Bishop Warburton criticised Wesley for seeing the hand of God in the accomodation of the breeze to the needs of an outdoor meeting. God may be seen in every benefit we receive, but enthusiasm consists " in believing those benefits to be miraculously conferred by a change in the established order of Nature." [2]

---

that " this infallible assurance does not so belong to the essence of faith, but that a true believer may wait long, and conflict with many difficulties before he be partaker of it." The doctrine of assurance was taught, at least implicitly, by the Church of England, as Wesley showed in his writings; but, in the eighteenth century, the doctrine was suspected of being connected with claims to special revelation. On the subject of the Methodist doctrine and its relations to historic theology, *vide* Herbert B. Workman, *The Place of Methodism in the Catholic Church* (London, 1921), chap. iii; J. G. Tasker, art. "Certainty" in *Encyclopedia of Religion and Ethics*.

[1] Quoted in Tyerman, *The Life of the Rev. George Whitefield*, vol. i, p. 220.

[2] Warburton, *op. cit.,* pp. 175-176.

No small part of the charge of enthusiastic claims to infallibility which Gibson and others brought against the Methodists was directed against itinerant preaching. Lecky long ago noticed the peculiar offensiveness to the established clergy of the irregular methods of the Methodists, who entered parishes uninvited, acted as missionaries of a neglected gospel and carried on open-air meetings which in the suspicious nostrils of the prelates smelled of conventicles.[1] Wesley himself entered into field-preaching with reluctance, and with even more hesitation began to employ lay helpers.

The latter action involved a defence of preaching by inward rather than by outward authority, and called down the accusation that the Methodists depended upon immediate inspiration for the substance of their discourses. As a result, in a passage against lay-preaching, Theophilus Evans saw as the consequences of Methodism the evils so freely pointed out in the days of the Commonwealth:

Their encouraging any illiterate Mechanick, that has but Assurance enough to ramble from Place to Place, as Exhortors and to expound Scripture, has very bad Consequences. In the particular Trade any of these was brought up, Taylor, Tinker, Weaver &c. he might be useful, and earn his Bread in an honest Way; but, growing idle and self-conceited, the general Method is to turn Exhortor. And, what is most shocking, every one of these illiterate Vagrants pretends to expound by Inspiration, and, which is rank Blasphemy, fathers all his crude Conceptions on the Dictates of the holy Spirit.[2]

The foregoing paragraphs illustrate the charges of enthusiasm which were brought against the early Methodists. Some of these charges are related to the conceptions of enthusiasm which were widespread in the early eighteenth cen-

---
[1] Lecky, *History of England in the Eighteenth Century* (London, 1878-1890), vol. ii, pp. 560-1.
[2] Evans, *The History of Modern Enthusiasm*, p. 116.

tury and which go back to the disturbances of the Commonwealth. Others have to do with the fundamental religious question of man's relation to the Deity. The latter type of charges was called out by the Methodist doctrines of conversion, assurance of salvation and of the Christian life. There remains to be determined the position of John Wesley himself in regard to enthusiasm, in its original meaning of immediate inspiration.

In regard to the extraordinary gifts of the Spirit, which include miracle, Wesley denied that they had ceased with the early church:

> Yet I do not know that God hath anyway precluded himself from thus exerting his sovereign power, from working miracles in any kind or degree, in any age, to the end of the world. I do not recollect any scripture wherein we are taught, that miracles were to be confined within the limits either of the apostolic or the Cyprianic age; or of any period of time, longer or shorter, even till the restitution of all things.[1]

The extraordinary gifts had not, indeed, persisted much beyond the first two or three centuries; but they ceased because the love of many had grown cold.[2] But Wesley agreed that, whether these gifts were designed to remain forever in the church or not, they were not given to all, perhaps not to one in a thousand.[3] His interest was always with the ordinary gifts, love, joy, peace and the like.

As already appears, Wesley had been accused of enthusiasm because of the emotional experiences attending his early meetings. Methodically he answered objectors, displaying an interest in "symptoms" which might indicate distraught

[1] *The Principles of a Methodist Farther Explained* (1746) in *Works*, vol. viii, p. 465.

[2] Sermon lxxxix, "The More Excellent Way," *Works*, vol. vii, p. 27.

[3] Wesley's *Standard Sermons*, vol. i, pp. 92-3, Sermon iv, "Scriptural Christianity."

minds. In March, 1743, he concluded a round of visiting in which he had particularly inquired into the "case of those who had almost every night the last week cried out aloud during the preaching."[1] He found that they were in perfect health and not subject to fits. They had all dropped down in a moment, without previous warning, seized with violent pain.

This they expressed in different manners. Some said they felt just as if a sword was running through them; others, that they thought a great weight lay upon them, as if it would squeeze them into the earth. Some said they were quite choked, so that they could not breathe; others, that their hearts swelled ready to burst; and others that it was as if their hearts, as if their inside, as if their whole body, was tearing all to pieces.[2]

This Wesley attributed to Satan tearing them,[3] and in another instance he objected strenuously, if somewhat pedantically, to being called an enthusiast because he had ascribed a woman's ravings to the power of the devil.[4]

But whereas in 1743 Wesley could no more attribute such symptoms "to any natural cause than to the Spirit of God,"[5] two years later he expressed a belief that his interest in physical symptoms had already implied. "I look upon some of these cases," he wrote, "as wholly natural; on the rest as mixed, both the disorder and the removal being partly natural and partly not."[6]

[1] *Journal,* vol. iii, p. 69.

[2] *Ibid.*

[3] *Ibid.*

[4] *An Answer to the Rev. Mr. Church's Remarks on the Rev. Mr. John Wesley's Last Journal* (1744-5) in *Works,* vol. viii, p. 408.

[5] *Journal,* vol. iii, p. 69.

[6] *An Answer to the Rev. Mr. Church's Remarks, Works,* vol. viii, p. 410.

In spite of his denials, opponents cited instances where Wesley seemed to have claimed immediate inspiration. All these he answered in methodical fashion, adding thereby to the store of unreadable books. But most of these charges related to miracles, to claims to special providence, to extraordinary favors from the Almighty; few had to do with enthusiasm in the ancient sense. That Wesley sometimes ascribed fits to demonic possession, occasionally cast lots and was otherwise superstitious need not be denied even by his best friends; but there is no reason to doubt that his sober judgment was expressed to Bishop Butler in 1739: " I pretend to no extraordinary revelations, or gifts of the Holy Ghost. None but what every Christian may receive and ought to expect and pray for." [1]

In his sermon on " The Nature of Enthusiasm," Wesley expressly names as enthusiasts those who imagine themselves to have gifts of God such as prophecy and working miracles, and others who in preaching or praying believe themselves influenced by the Holy Ghost as they are not. " Of this number, I fear, are all they who imagine that God dictates the very words they speak; and that, consequently, it is impossible they should speak anything amiss, either as to the matter or manner of it." [2] To these enthusiasts he adds those who expect to be directed in extraordinary manner by visions, dreams or strong impulsions on the mind.[3]

Nevertheless it remains true that Wesley's fundamental doctrines assumed man's immediate experience of God.[4] Assuming this experience of God as a fact, Wesley was put to

[1] Henry Moore, *The Life of the Rev. John Wesley, A.M.* (New York, 1826), vol. i, p. 269.

[2] *Standard Sermons,* vol. ii, pp. 94-5.

[3] *Ibid.,* p. 96.

[4] On the essentials of Methodist doctrine, *vide* Herbert B. Workman, *The Place of Methodism in the Catholic Church.*

it to explain how this could happen, since he rejected the mystic's explanation that man has within him an inner light which may be fanned into a flame, or a seed of the divine which will grow if properly tended. Although he had been early under the influence of William Law, Wesley would have nothing to do with that mystic's later devotion to Jacob Boehme. The mystics Wesley rejected because they slighted the church, with its ordinances and works of piety, indulged in unscriptural speculation and allowed tempers and words which did not seem either scriptural or social.[1] Wesley was left to the contemporary theological view of human nature, that it is corrupt and can produce of itself no good thing.

"Prevenient grace" helped Wesley over part of his difficulty, but salvation for him had to be a supernatural process, dependent upon faith;[2] and faith he defines as

... a power wrought by the Almighty in an immortal spirit, inhabiting a house of clay, to see through that veil into the world of spirits, into things invisible and eternal; a power to discern those things which with eyes of flesh and blood no man hath seen or can see, either by reason of their nature, which (though they surround us on every side) is not perceivable by these gross senses; or by reason of their distance, as being yet afar off in the bosom of eternity.[3]

Devoted to Locke's explanation of natural knowledge, Wesley had to posit a supernatural source for this spiritual discernment, since it is necessary that man have ideas of the things of God which are "fixed, distinct, and determinate:"

And seeing our ideas are not innate, but must all originally come from our senses, it is certainly necessary that you have senses capable of discerning objects of this kind: not those only

[1] *Journal*, vol. v, p. 46.
[2] *Standard Sermons*, vol. i, p. 41.
[3] *A Letter to the Rev. Dr. Conyers Middleton, Works*, vol. x, p. 73.

which are called natural senses ... but spiritual senses, exercised to discern spiritual good and evil. It is necessary that you have *the hearing ear* and the *seeing eye,* emphatically so called; that you have a new class of senses opened in your soul, not depending on organs of the flesh and blood, to be " the evidence of things not seen," as your bodily senses are of visible things; to be the avenues to the invisible world, to discern spiritual objects, and to furnish you with ideas of what the outward " eye hath not seen, neither the ear heard." [1]

For the present purpose there is no need to enter into the debate which Wesley carried on over the instantaneous character of conversion and sanctification; it is more pertinent to inquire what Wesley actually meant by the supernatural spiritual sense which he declared to be given in conversion. Obviously, if his statement is allowed to stand without explanation, Wesley has only presented Barclay's theory in the active voice.[2]

In the *Earnest Appeal,* Wesley does seem to expect that the converted will receive ideas by his spiritual sense just as " sensible ideas " are received by " external sensation." " So you cannot reason concerning spiritual things, if you have no spiritual sight; " he insists, " because all your ideas received by your outward senses are of a different kind; yea, far more different from those received by faith or internal sensation, than the idea of colour from that of sound." [3] But when one asks what ideas are received by " internal sensation," the answer seems to be that faith is only a " sure trust and confidence that God hath and will forgive our sins, that He hath accepted us again into His favour for the mer-

---

[1] Wesley, *An Earnest Appeal to Men of Reason and Religion, Works,* vol. viii, p. 13. *Cf.* Sermon xxxix, " The New Birth," especially II, 4, *Standard Sermons,* vol. ii, pp. 232-4.

[2] *Vide supra,* p. 91 n, for Barclay's theory.

[3] *Works,* vol. viii, pp. 13-14.

its of Christ's death and passion." [1] In similar fashion, Wesley restricts his doctrine of assurance.

In his famous sermon on "The Witness of the Spirit," written it would seem in 1746, Wesley elaborated the doctrine, which in the form in which it appears is often said to be his distinctive contribution to theology.[2] Here he contended for an immediate witness of the Holy Spirit to the individual, which is "an inward impression on the soul, whereby the Spirit of God directly witnesses to my spirit, that I am a child of God; that Jesus Christ hath loved me, and given Himself for me; and that all my sins are blotted out, and I, even I, am reconciled to God." [3]

Such a doctrine drew the epithet, enthusiast, even from bishops,[4] but Wesley was little moved, although he admitted that French Prophets and others might have claimed and even experienced the witness of the Spirit.[5] He seems to have changed his mind as to the necessity of Christians possessing "full assurance," [6] but he continued to preach his distinctive doctrine to the end of his life, safeguarding it only by insisting that this "direct" witness of the Spirit must be supplemented by the witness of one's own conscience, by the "fruits of the Spirit."

Wesley was shifting the emphasis in religion from external facts to inner experience, and he recognized the value of this for Christian apologetics. In answering Middleton on miracles, Wesley pointed out the weakness of the orthodox cause as it was then being defended:

---

[1] "Justification by Faith," iv, 3, *Standard Sermons*, vol. i, pp. 125-6.
[2] *Cf.* Tasker, art. "Certainty" in *Encyclopedia of Religion and Ethics*.
[3] *Standard Sermons*, vol. i, p. 208.
[4] *Cf.* Sugden, *Standard Sermons*, vol. i, p. 203n.
[5] *Ibid.*, vol. ii, pp. 352-3.
[6] *Ibid.*, vol. i, p. 201.

I have sometimes been almost inclined to believe, that the wisdom of God has, in most later ages, permitted the external evidence of Christianity to be more or less clogged and incumbered for this very end, that men (of reflection especially) might not altogether rest there, but be constrained to look into themselves also, and attend to the light shining in their hearts . . .

Without this I cannot but doubt, whether they can long maintain their cause; whether if they do not obey the loud call of God, and lay far more stress than they have hitherto done on this internal evidence of Christianity, they will not, one after another, give up the external, and (in heart at least) go over to those whom they are now contending with; so that in a century or two the people of England will be fairly divided into real Deists and real Christians.[1]

Notwithstanding the value of this appeal to inward experience, Wesley was unwilling to substitute the experience of the individual for external authorities. His practical sense heightened by the problems of administration in his societies forced him to clear definition of the guides for conduct. He had said that faith, defined as supernatural spiritual discernment, " resolves a thousand enigmas of the highest concern; "[2] and thus stumbled once more into the whole question of knowledge gained by immediate inspiration. Moreover, he could not bring himself to deny that one *might* receive mental impressions which should serve as guidance in practical affairs, and he quotes with approval some " great man " who observed:

that there is a three-fold leading of the Spirit: some he leads by giving them on every occasion apposite texts of Scripture; some by suggesting reasons for every step they take [" the way by which he leads me," added Wesley] and some by impressions; but he judges the last to be the least desirable way, as it is often

[1] *Letter to the Rev. Dr. Middleton, Works,* vol. x, pp. 76-7.
[2] *Ibid.,* vol. x, p. 75.

impossible to distinguish dark impressions from divine, or even diabolical.[1]

Such general statements did not suffice, however, when confronted with his societies and with the attacks of opponents. In reply to Thomas Church, Wesley denied following " secret impulses " himself:

> I have declared again and again, that I make the word of God the rule of all my actions; and that I no more follow any secret impulses instead thereof, than I follow Mohammed or Confucius.
>
> > Not even a word or look,
> > Do I approve or own,
> > But by the model of thy book
> > Thy sacred book alone.[2]

Human actions and doctrines must be tested not only by the Bible but also by reason. In answering another opponent, Wesley said:

> For " reason " you say, " cannot do much with an enthusiast, whose first principle is, to have nothing to do with reason, but resolve all his religious opinions and notions into immediate inspiration." Then, by your own account, I am no enthusiast: for I resolve none of my notions into immediate inspiration.... And I am ready to give up every opinion which I cannot by calm, clear, reason defend.[3]

---

[1] Letter to Freeborn Garretson, dated July 15, 1789, quoted in Nathan Bangs, *Life of the Rev. Freeborn Garretson*. . . . (New York, 1829), p. 196.

[2] *Answer to the Rev. Mr. Church, Works,* vol. viii, p. 406. The quotation is from George Herbert, *The Temple,* " Discipline ":

> > Not a word or look
> > I affect to own,
> > But by book,
> > And thy book alone.

[3] *Letter to the Rev. Mr. Downes, Works,* vol. ix, p. 105.

Wesley was not content to leave his followers to regulate their conduct by the Bible and by reason; he added thereto a system of supervision which has rarely been equalled in Christian history. His converts were organized into "societies," with leaders who were responsible to such helpers as Wesley chose to send out, and ultimately to Wesley himself. Even a cursory reading of the "General Rules" of these societies will give some idea of the Methodist discipline. The members of the societies were expected to attend class meetings once a week at which time the leaders inquired about their souls and advised, reproved, comforted or exhorted them. The members were to do no harm, which was explained by several definite prohibitions, against swearing, drunkenness, "buying or selling uncustomed goods;" to do good, by charitable acts, evangelistic endeavor and pious lives; to attend "upon all the ordinances of God," such as public worship, private prayer, the Lord's Supper and reading the Scriptures.

It is evident that the individual Methodist was under such careful guidance that there was little danger of enthusiastic outbreaks sufficient to threaten the peace of the country. In even stricter fashion did Wesley safeguard his preachers. He had been influenced by reading, in 1746, the work of a dissenter, Lord King, *An Inquiry into the Constitution, Discipline, Unity, and Worship of the Primitive Church.* From that time, he seems to have accepted King's contention that elders and bishops are essentially of the same order.[1] On the matter of preaching by laymen, however, Wesley was moved by immediate necessity, his guide in most matters of practice. And this necessity caused him to admit lay helpers on the principle that they were called by the Holy Ghost. Here Wesley comes close to the prophetism of the early

[1] Tyerman, *op. cit.,* vol. i, p. 508 *et seq.*; on Wesley's idea of the church, *vide* Workman, *op. cit.,* chap. viii.

church; but Wesley retained his belief in ordination by the presbyters when the bishops would not act, and in the right of ordained ministers alone to administer the Sacraments. On the question of lay preachers, Wesley, in 1755, expressed himself clearly:

It is not clear to us that presbyters, so circumstanced as we are, may appoint, or ordain others; but it is, that we may direct, as well as suffer them to do, what we conceive they are moved to by the Holy Ghost. It is true that, in ordinary cases, both an inward and an outward call are requisite. But we apprehend, there is something far from ordinary in the present case. And, upon the calmest view of things, we think, they who are only called of God, and not of man, have more right to preach, than they who are only called of man, and not of God.[1]

Although Wesley sanctioned an immediate calling to the work of the ministry, he safeguarded this as he did his doctrine of direct guidance of individual Christians by the Holy Ghost. A Methodist preacher might be called of God to preach, but he did his work under the meticulous supervision of John Wesley. By him the preacher was directed what to read, what exercise to take, when to get up in the morning. His Rules of a Helper end with this admonition:

Act in all things, not according to your own will, but as a son in the Gospel. As such, it is your part to employ your time in the manner which we direct; partly, in preaching and visiting from house to house; partly, in reading, meditation, and prayer. Above all, if you labour with us in our Lord's vineyard, it is needful that you should do that part of the work which we advise, at those times and places which we judge most for his glory.[2]

[1] Letter to Thomas Adams, *Works*, vol. xiii, p. 208. Later Wesley did, of course, ordain several preachers.
[2] *Minutes of Some Late Conversations between the Rev. Mr. Wesley and Others, Works*, vol. viii, p. 310.

In explaining the origins of his system, Wesley carefully explained that he invited preachers to join him, that they came on his invitation and were at liberty to leave when they chose; but while they remained, there was no changing his rules. "Every Preacher and every member may leave me when he pleases. But while he chooses to stay, it is on the same terms that he joined me at first."[1]

Thus hedged about, Methodist preachers and people yet had plenty of opportunity to express their feelings. There were frequent preachings, weekly class meetings, meetings of leaders and helpers. In class the people could confess their sins, talk of their religious experience, discuss their problems, all within the bosom of the Methodist family. The helpers wrote out their spiritual autobiographies and sent them to Wesley, who pondered and duly printed them in his *Arminian Magazine*. The Methodists' services were themselves outlets for emotion. Even to-day in some places the name "noisy Methodists" testifies to a kind of meeting which has little resemblance to middle-class Methodism in American cities. For these meetings Charles Wesley wrote innumerable songs, some of them to lively tunes which scandalized good Churchmen; he once set a religious song to the tune of a musical-hall ditty called "Nancy Dawson."

Such was the character of Methodist "enthusiasm": unusual and disturbing religious practices carried on in defiance of "taste" and propriety and with joyous disregard of ecclesiastical law; an insistence upon immediate communion of the individual with God, restricted, however, to a change of the individual's inner life, a certainty of personal relation with the Deity, and to such experiences as did not conflict with the Bible or "Reason" and did not exceed the privileges of every Christian.

[1] *Works, op. cit.*, p. 313.

To estimate the place of Methodism in the history of enthusiasm, one must glance back at the troubled century which preceded the rise of the Wesleyan societies. Claims to immediate inspiration on the part of certain individuals and groups in the period between the Long Parliament and the establishment of the House of Hanover had aggravated the ancient fear of enthusiasm which arose out of the church's long experience with the "inspired." The wide-spread opposition, particularly on the part of Churchmen, to the early Methodists is partly explained by this phobia. But the absence of organized persecution unto blood is testimony that Englishmen had come a long way since Cromwell's Council sat in solemn conference on the revelations of prophets. Theological, philosophical and scientific writers had produced some effect on popular thinking; and changes in economic and political problems had helped to form that indefinable something that we call public opinion. Men could laugh at or study, according to their bent, the enthusiasts whom their forefathers had feared.

Into this new situation Wesley came with his own often inconsistent theology. He admitted the possibility of immediate revelation, and would listen respectfully to the most boresome accounts of visions and inner impulses.[1] But practically, he so regulated this enthusiasm by doctrinal and organizational safeguards that the Methodist boasted, not of infallible information, but of conversion from vice to moral living and of assurance that he was a child of God. The result of this change was that the Methodists as a whole fell neither into the mystic's passive pietism nor into the enthusiast's unrestrained individualism. The emphasis of religious interest was shifted to experience, and a new apologetic was

[1] *Cf.* the long account of Grace Murray's religious experiences reprinted in the author's *The Lord's Horseman* (New York, 1928), pp. 279-315.

made possible. Since immediate touch with God was affirmed at the same time that personal infallibility was denied, it was possible for Methodism to become a great romantic religious movement, in which emotion was recognized as legitimate and was both cultivated and given expression. In public worship, in the confessional of class meetings, in mutual aid such as relief of poor, establishment of dispensaries, the visitation of the sick, the Methodists found an outlet for their emotional life which did not incur the danger of " new lights." This could not have happened when the fear of enthusiasm was upon the minds of men, nor could it have happened without the pragmatic genius of a Wesley.

In this creation of a romantic movement in religion that shifted the emphasis in the English-speaking world from authority to experience, Wesley spent his days. So effectually did he work that he himself lived to see the time when he was no longer met with episcopal denunciations and popular violence, and his spiritual descendants have lived to see him enshrined among the stained-glass saints of the Church that he loved but from which his followers separated, and to hear sober Churchmen debating whether Wesley was not the greatest man of his century.

In Methodism, then, English enthusiasm in the classic sense, came to an end. However it may remain embalmed in official creeds, practically the idea has passed away. Religion, if it choose, may base itself upon the inner life, even upon the emotions, without arousing the fear of the guardians of society. With this change has come a new emphasis in religion and a new apologetic. Unafraid of claims to direct inspiration, modern Christianity has concerned itself with psychological facts, and looks more and more to such contemporary evidence for the justification of religion. Enthusiasm has given way to experience.

BIBLIOGRAPHY

I. Reference Works [1]

Dictionnaire apologétique de la foi catholique. Edited by A. D'Alès, Paris, in process.
Dictionnaire de théologie catholique... Edited by A. Vacant and E. Mangenot, continued by E. Amann, Paris, 1909-.
Encyclopaedia Biblica. Edited by T. W. Cheyne and J. Sutherland Black, 4 vols., New York, 1899-1903.
Encyclopedia of Religion and Ethics, 12 vols., New York, 1911-1923.
A New English Dictionary on Historical Principles. Edited by James A. H. Murray, Oxford, 1888-1928, 10 vols.
Kirchenlexikon oder Encyklopädie der katholischen Theologie und ihrer Hülfswissenschaften. Second edition by J. Hergenröther and F. Kaulen, 12 vols., Freiburg im Breisgau, 1880-1901.
Realencyklopädie für protestantische Theologie und Kirche, third edition, 24 vols., Leipzig, 1896-1913.

II. Authorities for History of Enthusiasm to the Seventeenth Century [2]

Alanus ab Insulis, *De fide catholica contra haereticos sui temporis.* . . . (Migne, *Patrologia Latina,* vol. ccx).
Angus, Samuel, *The Mystery-Religions and Christianity,* New York, 1925.
The Ante-Nicene Fathers. Revised by A. Cleveland Coxe, 10 vols., New York, 1908-1913.
D'Aubigné, J. H. Merle, *History of the Reformation of the Sixteenth Century.* Translated by H. White, 5 vols., New York, 1853.
Augustine, *De divinatione daemonum (Corpus scriptorum ecclesiasticorum latinorum,* vol. xxxxi. Recensuit Josephus Zycha, Vienna, 1900).
Bax, E. Belfort, *Rise and Fall of the Anabaptists.* London and New York, 1903.
Benedict XIV, *De servorum dei beatificatione et beatorum canonizatione* . . . . 4 vols., Bononiae, 1734-1738.

---

[1] Such well-known works as the *Dictionary of National Biography,* the *Britannica* and the *Jewish* and *Catholic* encyclopaedias have been omitted.

[2] Omitting obvious authorities such as the *Cambridge Medieval* and *Cambridge Modern* histories.

Bevan, Edwyn, *Sibyls and Sages,* London, 1928.
Beveridge, W., art., "Joachim of Floris," in *Encyclopedia of Religion and Ethics.*
Bouché-Leclercq, A., *Histoire de la divination dans l'antiquité,* 4 vols., Paris, 1879-1882.
Brueys, M. de, *Histoire du fanatisme de notre tems.* . . . 3 vols. in 1. Utrecht, 1737.
Burnet, Gilbert, *The History of the Reformation of the Church of England.* A new edition . . . by Nicholas Pocock, M.A., 7 vols., Oxford, 1865.
Caird, Edward, *The Evolution of Theology in the Greek Philosophers,* 2 vols., Glasgow, 1904. (Gifford Lectures, 1900-1901, 1901-1902.)
Calvin, John, *Institution de la religion chrétienne,* reimpriemeé sous la direction d'A. Lefranc par H. Chatelain et J. Pannier, Paris, 1911.
——, *Institutes of the Christian Religion.* Translated by John Allen, 4 vols., Philadelphia, 1909.
Chapman, John, art., "Mysticism: Christian, Roman Catholic," in *Encyclopedia of Religion and Ethics.*
M. Tulli Ciceronis scripta quae manserunt omnia, recognovit C. F. W. Mueller, pars iv, vol. ii, Leipzig, 1878.
M. Tulli Ciceronis de divinatione. Liber Primus. Edited by Arthur Stanley Pease. The University of Illinois, 1920. (University of Ill. Studies in Language and Literature, vol. vi, no. 2, May, 1920; vol. vi, no. 3, Aug., 1920.)
M. Tulli Ciceronis de divinatione. Liber Secundus. Edited by Arthur Stanley Pease. The University of Illinois, 1923. (Univ. of Ill. Studies in Language and Literature, vol. viii, no. 2, May, 1923; Aug., 1923.)
Corpus juris canonici, post curas A. L. Richteri instruxit Aemilius Friedberg, second Leipzig edition, 2 vols., Leipzig, 1879-1881.
Cumont, Franz, *Oriental Religions in Roman Paganism,* Chicago, 1911.
Davidson, A. B., *The Theology of the Old Testament,* New York, 1914.
Döllinger, J. J. L. von, *Kleinere Schriften,* Stuttgart, 1890.
——, *Fables respecting the popes in the Middle Ages translated by Alfred Plummer* . . . . *together with* . . . . *The Prophetic Spirit and the Prophecies of the Christian Era, translated* . . . *by Henry B. Smith,* D.D., New York, 1872.
——, *Beiträge zur Sektengeschichte des Mittelalters,* 2 vols., München, 1890.
Dorner, J. A., *History of Protestant Theology.* Translated by George Robson, M.A., 2 vols., Edinburgh, 1871.
Dosker, H. E., "Recent Sources of Information on the Anabaptists in the Netherlands," in *Papers of the American Society of Church History,* second series, vol. v, New York and London, 1917.

BIBLIOGRAPHY

Doumergue, E., *Jean Calvin. Les hommes et les choses de son temps,* 7 vols., Lausanne, 1899-1927.

Drummond, James, *Philo Judaeus; or the Jewish Alexandrian Philosophy in its Development and Completion,* 2 vols., London, 1888.

Du Plessis d'Argentré, Charles, *Collectio judiciorum de novis erroribus, qui ab initio duodecimi seculi post Incarnationem Verbi usque ad annum 1632 in Ecclesia prescripti sunt & notati* . . . . 2 vols., Lutetiae Parisiorum, 1728.

Euripides with an English Translation, London and New York, 1912 (Loeb Classical Library).

Eymeric, Nicholas, *Directorium inquisitorum cum commentariis* . . . . Venetiis, 1607.

Fairweather, William, *The Background of the Gospels,* Edinburgh, 1908.

Farnell, L. R., *The Cults of the Greek States,* 5 vols., Oxford, 1896-1899.

Fowler, W. Warde, *The Religious Experience of the Roman People from the earliest times to the Age of Augustus,* London, 1911 (Gifford Lectures, 1909-1910).

Gebhart, Emile, *Mystics and Heretics in Italy.* Translated by E. M. Hulme, London, 1922.

Gerson, Jean, *Opera Omnia,* Antwerp, 1706, 5 vols., fol.

Glover, T. R., *The Conflict of Religions in the Early Roman Empire,* eighth edition, London, 1919.

Grisar, Hartmann, *Luther.* Trans. by E. M. Lamond, 6 vols. (London, 1917).

Gui, Bernard, *Practica inquisitionis* . . . . Edited by C. Douais, Paris, 1886.

Hahn, Christoph Ulrich, *Geschichte der Ketzer im Mittelalter, besonders im 11., 12. und 13. Jahrhundert, nach den Quellen Bearbeitet,* 3 vols., Stuttgart, 1845-1850.

Hallam, Henry, *Introduction to the Literature of Europe in the Fifteenth, Sixteenth, and Seventeenth Centuries,* 4 vols. in 2, New York, 1894 (Parts iii and iv deal with the seventeenth century).

Hansen, Joseph. *Zauberwahn. Inquisition, und Hexenprozess im Mittelalter und die Entstehung der grossen Hexenverfolgung,* München and Leipzig, 1900 (Historische Bibliothek, Band xii).

Hardwick, Charles, *A History of the Articles of Religion,* Philadelphia, 1860.

Harnack, Adolph, *History of Dogma.* Translated from the third edition by Neil Buchanan, 7 vols., Boston, 1905.

Harrison, Jane Ellen, *Prolegomena to the Study of Greek Religion,* second edition, Cambridge, 1908.

Hatch, William Henry Paine, *The Pauline Idea of Faith in its Relation to Jewish and Hellenistic Religion,* Cambridge (U.S.A.), 1917.

Hefele, Karl Joseph von, *Histoire des conciles* .... *traduction français faite sur la deuxième édition allemande* .... *aug. de notes critiques et bibliographiques, par* .... [Henri Leclercq] .... 8 vols., Paris, 1907-1921.
Herrmann, Wilhelm, *The Communion of the Christian with God,* English translation, Oxford, 1895.
Ieiler, Ign., art., " Privatoffenbarungen," *Kirchenlexikon oder Encyklopädie der katholischen Theologie und ihrer Hülfswissenschaften.*
Inge, William Ralph, *The Philosophy of Plotinus,* second edition, 2 vols., London, 1923 (Gifford Lectures, 1917-1918).
Jackson, F. J. Foakes and Kirsopp Lake [eds.], *The Beginnings of Christianity,* 3 vols., London, 1920-1926.
Jowett, Benjamin, *The Dialogues of Plato translated into English with analyses and introduction,* third edition, 5 vols., New York and London, n.d. (copyright, 1892).
Kennedy, H. A. A., *St. Paul and the Mystery Religions,* London, n.d. (preface dated 1915).
Köstlin, Julius, *Martin Luther, sein Leben und seine Schriften.* Fünfte neubearbeitete Auflage, nach des Verfassers Tode fortgesetzt von D. Gustav Kawerau, 2 vols., Berlin, 1903.
Lake, Kirsopp, *The Earlier Epistles of St. Paul,* London, 1911.
——, *The Apostolic Fathers with an English Translation,* 2 vols., London and New York, 1913 (The Loeb Classical Library).
Lawlor, Hugh Jackson, art., " Montanism" in *Encyclopedia of Religion and Ethics.*
Lea, Henry Charles, *A History of the Inquisition of the Middle Ages,* 3 vols., New York, 1888.
Leisegang, Hans, *Der Heilige Geist. Das Wesen und Werden der Mystisch-Intuitiven Erkenntnis in der Philosophie und Religion der Griechen,* I Band, I Teil, Leipzig und Berlin, 1919.
Lewy, Hans, *Sobria Ebrietas: Untersuchungen zur Geschichte der antiken Mystik,* Giessen, 1929.
Library, A Select, of the Nicene and Post-Nicene Fathers of the Christian Church. Edited by Philip Schaff, 14 vols., New York, 1899-1914.
——, *A New Series,* 14 vols., New York, 1890-1912.
Limborch, Philipp à, *Historia inquisitionis cui subjungitur liber sententiarum inquisitionis Tholosanae ab anno Christo 1307 ad annum 1323,* 2 vols., Amstelodami, 1692.
Lindsay, Thomas M., *The Church and the Ministry in the Early Centuries,* London, n.d. (preface dated 1905, in second edition).
——, *A History of the Reformation,* second edition, 2 vols., New York, 1912 and 1917.
Luther, Martin, *Widder de hymelischen propheten von den bildern und Sacrament Martinus Luther Ihre torheyt wird yderman offinbar*

BIBLIOGRAPHY

werden, 2. Timoth. 3. Gedruckt zu Wittenberg [1524] (British Museum copy).
——, *Das ander Teyl widder die hymlischen propheten vom Sacrament. Martinus Luther. Ihr Torheyt wird yderman offinbar werden, 2. Timoth. 3. Gedruck zu Wittenberg* [1524?] (British Museum copy).
——, *Werke, Kritische Gesammtausgabe,* Weimar, 1883, in progress.
McGiffert, Arthur Cushman, *Protestant Thought Before Kant,* New York, 1911.
Mangenot, E., art., "Inspiration de L'Ecriture," *Dictionnaire de Théologie Catholique.*
Mansi, Giovanni Domenico, *Sacrorum conciliorum nova et amplissima collectio* . . . . 53 vols., Florentiae, etc., 1759-1927.
Meersch, J. Van der, art., "Grace," *Dictionnaire de Théologie Catholique.*
Moneta, *Adversus Catharos et Valdenses libri quinque* . . . Romae, 1743.
Moore, George Foote, *History of Religions,* 2 vols., London, 1913-1919.
——, *Judaism,* 3 vols., Cambridge (U. S. A.), 1927-30.
More, Paul Elmer, *The Religion of Plato,* Princeton, 1921.
Murray, Gilbert, *Five Stages of Greek Religion,* New York, 1925.
Muzzey, David Saville, *The Spiritual Franciscans,* New York, 1907.
Ortolan, T., art., "Démoniaques," *Dictionnaire de Théologie Catholique.*
Peucer, Caspar, *Commentarius De Praecipuis Divinationum generibus, in quo a prophetiis divina authoritate traditis, et Physicis praedictionibus, separantur Diabolicae, fraudes & superstitiosae observationes, & explicantur fontes ac causae Physicarum praedictionum, Diabolicae et superstitiosae confutatae damnantur, ea serie, quam tabula indicis vice praefixa ostendit* . . . . *Wittenbergae M.D.LIII.*
Pohle, Joseph, art., "Grace," *Catholic Encyclopedia.*
Reformatio Legum Ecclesiasticarum . . . . London, 1571.
Reitzenstein, R., *Die Hellenistischen Mysterienreligionen nach ihren Grundgedanken und Wirkungen* . . . . Zweite umgearbeitete Auflage, Berlin, 1920.
Rohde, Erwin, *Psyche: Seelencult und Unsterblichkeitsglaube der Griechen.* Zweite verbesserte Auflage, Freiburg i.B., 1898, 2 Bände.
Rohr, Ignaz, "Die Prophetie in letzten Jahrhundert vor der Reformation als Geschichtsquelle und Geschichtsfaktor." *Historisches Jahrbuch,* vol. xix (1898), pp. 29-56; 547-566 [misnumbered 447-466].
Schaff, Phillip [ed.], *The Creeds of Christendom,* 3 vols., New York, 1877-1881.
Schmiedel, Paul W., art., "Spiritual Gifts" in *Encyclopaedia Biblica.*
Scott, Ernest F., *The Spirit in the New Testament,* New York, n.d. (preface dated 1923).
Smith, George Adam, *The Book of the Twelve Prophets,* New York, n.d. (The Expositor's Bible).
Smith, Preserved, *The Life and Letters of Martin Luther,* Boston and New York, 1911.

———, *The Age of the Reformation*, New York, 1920.

Sprenger, Jacob and Kraemer, H., *Malleus Maleficarum in tres divisus partes, In quibus concurrentia ad maleficia, Maleficiorum effectus, Remedia adversus maleficia, Et modus denique procedendi, ac puniendi Maleficos abundé continetur, praecipue autem omnibus Inquisitoribus, & divini Verbi Concionatoribus Utilis, ac necessarius* . . . . Francofurti ad Moenum, M.D.LXXX.

———, *Malleus Maleficarum* translated with an Introduction, Bibliography and Notes by the Rev. Montague Summers, London, 1928.

Stevens, George Barker, *The Theology of the New Testament*, New York, 1916.

Swete, Henry Barclay, *The Holy Spirit in the New Testament*, London, 1919.

Tambornino, Julius, *De antiquorum daemonismo*, Giessen, 1909, (Dieterich & Wuensch, *Religionsgeschichtliche Versuche und Vorarbeiten*, Band 7, Heft. 3).

Thorndike, Lynn, *Magic and Experimental Science in the First Thirteen Centuries of our Era*, 2 vols., New York, 1923.

Toy, Crawford Howell, *Judaism and Christianity*, Boston, 1892.

Troeltsch, Ernst, art., " Calvin " in *Hibbert Journal*, vol. viii, pp. 102-121.

Taylor, Henry Osborn, *The Medieval Mind*, second edition, 2 vols., London, 1914.

Thomas Aquinas, *Opera Omnia iussu impensaque Leonis XIII P. M. Edita* . . . . Rome, 1882, in progress.

Vernet, F., " Frères du Libre Esprit," *Dictionnaire de Théologie Catholique*.

Warfield, B. B., *Counterfeit Miracles*, New York, 1918.

Watkin-Jones, Howard, *The Holy Spirit in the Medieval Church*, London, 1922.

Wendland, Paul, *Die Hellenistisch-Römische Kultur in ihren Beziehungen zu Judentum und Christentum*, Zweite und Dritte Auflage, Tubingen, 1912.

White, Andrew Dickson, *A History of the Warfare of Science with Theology in Christendom*, 2 vols., New York, 1897.

Yonge, C. D., *The Works of Philo Judaeus* . . . . *translated from the Greek*, 4 vols., London, 1854-1855.

III. ENGLAND IN THE SEVENTEENTH AND EIGHTEENTH CENTURIES

I. POLITICAL AND SOCIAL HISTORY [1]

Berens, Lewis H., *The Digger Movement in the Days of the Commonwealth*, London, 1906.

[1] Pepys, Evelyn, Clarendon and other familiar sources are omitted. Wherever reference has been made to these, the edition used has been indicated in footnotes.

Bernstein, Eduard, "Kommunistisch und demokratisch-Sozialistische Strömungen während der englischen Revolution des 17. Jahrhunderts" in *Die Geschichte des Sozialismus in Einzeldarstellungen.* Erster Band, Zweiter Theil, Stuttgart, 1875.

Brown, Louise Fargo, *The Political Activities of the Baptists and Fifth Monarchy Men in England during the Interregnum,* London, 1912.

Burnet, Gilbert, *History of My Own Times.* Edited by Osmund Airy, 2 vols., Oxford, 1897-1900.

Cunningham, William, *The Growth of English Industry and Commerce in Modern Times,* fifth edition, 3 vols., Cambridge, 1910-1912.

Davies, Geoffrey, *Bibliography of British History. Stuart Period, 1605-1714,* Oxford, 1928.

Firth, Charles Harding [ed.], *The Clarke Papers,* vols. i and ii, London, 1891 and 1894 (Camden Society).

——, *The Last Years of the Protectorate, 1656-1658,* 2 vols., London, 1909.

——, and Rait, R. S. [eds.], *Acts and Ordinances of the Interregnum,* 3 vols., London, 1911.

Gardiner, S. R., *History of the Great Civil War, 1642-1649,* 4 vols., London, 1893.

——, *The History of the Commonwealth and Protectorate,* 4 vols., London, 1903.

Hume, David, *The History of England,* New York, 1879.

Leadam, L. S., *The History of England from the Accession of Anne to the Death of George III,* London, 1912.

Lecky, William Edward Hartpole, *A History of England in the Eighteenth Century,* 8 vols., New York, 1878-1890.

Lodge, Richard, *The History of England from the Restoration to the Death of William III,* London, 1912.

Montague, F. C., *The History of England from the Accession of James I to the Restoration,* London, 1916.

Morgan, William Thomas, *English Political Parties and Leaders in the Reign of Queen Anne, 1702-1710,* New Haven, 1920.

Pease, Theodore Calvin, *The Leveller Movement,* Washington, 1916.

Sydney, W. C., *England and the English in the Eighteenth Century,* 2 vols., London, 1892.

Traill, H. D. and Mann, J. S. [eds.], *Social England,* 12 vols., London, 1909.

Trevelyan, G. M., *England under the Stuarts,* New York and London, 1904.

——, *England under Queen Anne, Blenheim,* London, 1930.

2. ECCLESIASTICAL HISTORY

Abbey, Charles J., *The English Church and its Bishops, 1700-1800,* 2 vols., London, 1887.

BIBLIOGRAPHY

Allut, Jean, account of mission of French Prophets (from London) to Germany, in short manuscript transcribed in article entitled "French Prophets of 1711," in *The Baptist Quarterly incorporating the Transactions of the Baptist Historical Society,* New Series, vol. ii, no. 4 (October, 1924), pp. 169-179.

Assembly of Divines, *The Humble Advice of the Assembly of Divines, by Authority of Parliament sitting at Westminster; concerning a Confession of Faith: With the Quotations and Texts of Scriptures annexed. Presented by them lately to both Houses of Parliament: now Published with Scriptures at Length, for the good of Families,* London .... *1658.*

Baird, Henry Martyn, "The Camisard Uprising of the French Protestants," *Papers of the American Society of Church History,* vol. ii, part i (New York, 1890), pp. 13-34.

Barclay, Robert, *The Inner Life of the Religious Societies of the Commonwealth,* London, 1876.

Bast, Charles, "Les Prophètes du Languedoc in 1701 et 1702," in *Revue Historique,* t. xxvi, 270.

Baxter, Richard, *Reliquiae Baxterianae: or Mr. Richard Baxter's Narrative of the Most Memorable Passages of his Life and Times. Faithfully publish'd from his own Original Manuscript by Matthew Sylvester ....* London .... *1696.*

Braithwaite, William Charles, *Spiritual Guidance in the Experience of Society of Friends,* London, 1909.

——, *The Beginnings of Quakerism,* London, 1912.

——, *The Second Period of Quakerism,* London, 1919.

Burrage, Champlin, *The Early English Dissenters in the Light of Recent Research (1550-1641),* 2 vols., Cambridge, 1912.

Calamy, Edmund, *The Principles and Practices of Moderate Non-conformists with Respect to Ordination Exemplify'd. . . . To which is Added, a Letter to a Divine in Germany, giving a Brief but True Account of the Protestant Dissenters in England . . .* London *. . . 1717.*

Clark, H. W., *History of English Nonconformity,* 2 vols., London, 1913.

Crosby, Thomas, *History of the English Baptists,* 4 vols., London, 1738-1740.

Dale, R. W., *History of English Congregationalism,* London, 1907.

Fry, John, *An Alphabetical Extract of all the Annual printed Epistles which have been sent to the several Quarterly meetings of the People call'd Quakers, in England and elsewhere, from their Yearly-Meetings in London .... from the Year 1682 to 1762 inclusive,* London, n.d. (preface dated 1762).

Gee, H. and Hardy, W. J. [eds.], *Documents Illustrative of English Church History,* London, 1896.

Gwatkin, Henry Melvill, *Church and State in England to the Death of Queen Anne*, London, 1917.
Heath, R., " The Little Prophets of the Cevennes," *Contemporary Review*, Jan., 1886.
Hetherington, W. M., *History of the Westminster Assembly of Divines*, fourth edition, Edinburgh, 1878.
Hodgkin, Thomas, *George Fox*, third edition, London, 1906.
Hutton, William Holden, *The English Church from the Accession of Charles II to the Death of Anne (1625-1714)*, London, 1913 (vol. vi of *A History of the English Church* edited by W. R. W. Stephens and William Hunt).
Inge, William Ralph, *Studies of English Mystics*, London, 1907.
Ivimey, Joseph, *A History of the English Baptists*, 4 vols., London, 1811.
Jessop, Augustus, *The Coming of the Friars and other Historical Essays*, London, 1913.
Jones, Rufus M., *Studies in Mystical Religion*, London, 1909.
——, *Spiritual Reformers in the 16th and 17th Centuries*, London, 1914.
Neal, Daniel, *The History of the Puritans*, 4 vols., London, 1732-1738.
Newman, Albert Henry, art., " Baptists," *Encyclopaedia Britannica*.
Nightingale, Benjamin, *Early Stages of the Quaker Movement in Lancashire*, London, n.d. (preface dated 1921).
Overton, John Henry and Abbey, Charles J., *The English Church in the Eighteenth Century*, 2 vols., London, 1878.
Overton, John Henry, *The Life and Opinions of William Law*, London, 1881.
——, *The Nonjurors*, London, 1902.
Plummer, Alfred, *The Church of England in the Eighteenth Century*, London, 1910.
Sewel, William, *The History of the Rise, Increase, and Progress of the Christian People Called Quakers*, fourth edition, 2 vols., London, 1798-1800.
Sippell, Theodore, *Zur Vorgeschichte des Quakertums*, Giessen, 1920 (*Studien zur Geschichte des neueren Protestantismus*, 12 Heft).
Stoughton, John, *Religion in England under Queen Anne and the Georges, 1702-1800*, 2 vols., London, 1878.
Sykes, Norman, *Edmund Gibson, Bishop of London 1649-1748*, Oxford and London, 1926.
Taylor, Adam, *The History of the English General Baptists*, in two parts, 2 vols. in 1, London, 1818.
Telford, John, *A History of Lay Preaching in the Christian Church*, London, 1897.
Walton, Christopher, *Notes and Materials for an adequate Biography of William Law*, London, 1854.

3. INTELLECTUAL HISTORY: THEOLOGY, PHILOSOPHY, PUBLIC OPINION, ETC.

Bacon, Francis, *Advancement of Learning and Novum Organum.* With a special introduction by James Edward Creighton .... New York (copyright 1900).

Beers, Henry Augustus, *A History of English Romanticism in the Eighteenth Century,* New York, 1913.

Berkeley, George, *The Works of George Berkeley, D.D., formerly Bishop of Cloyne...Including his Posthumous Works.* Edited by Alexander Campbell Frazer, 4 vols., Oxford, 1901.

Bourne, H. R., *The Life of John Locke,* 2 vols., London, 1876.

Brett, George Sidney, *A History of Psychology,* vol. ii, London and New York, 1921.

Burton, John Hill, *Life and Correspondence of David Hume,* 2 vols, Edinburgh, 1846.

Butler, Joseph, *The Analogy of Religion,* London, 1886 (first edition, 1736).

Carlyle, Thomas, *Oliver Cromwell's Letters and Speeches.* Edited by S. C. Lomas, 3 vols., London, 1904.

Chalmers, Alexander [ed.], *The Works of the English Poets,* 21 vols., London, 1810.

Courthope, W. J., *A History of English Poetry,* vol. v., London, 1919.

Cudworth, Ralph, *The True Intellectual System of the Universe.* Edited by J. L. Mosheim, 3 vols., London, 1845.

Culverwel, Nathaniel, *An Elegant and Learned Discourse of the Light of Nature,* London, 1662.

Dennis, John, *A Large Account of the Taste in Poetry* (1702) reprinted in Durham, *Critical Essays,* pp. 113-142.

Durham, William Higley [ed.], *Critical Essays of the Eighteenth Century 1700-1725,* New Haven, London, Oxford, 1915.

Figgis, J. Neville, *The Theory of the Divine Rights of Kings,* Cambridge, 1896.

Flynn, John Stephen, *The Influence of Puritanism on the Political and Religious Thought of the English,* London, 1920.

Forster, Thomas, *Original Letters of Locke, Algernon Sidney, and Anthony Lord Shaftesbury,* London, 1830.

Gibson, James, *Locke's Theory of Knowledge and its Historical Relations,* Cambridge, 1912.

Gillett, Charles R. [ed.], *Catalogue of the McAlpin Collection,* 5 vols., New York, 1927-1930.

Gooch, George Peabody, *The History of English Democratic Ideas in the Seventeenth Century,* Cambridge, 1898.

Greenslet, Ferris, *Joseph Glanville, a Study in English Thought and Letters in the Seventeenth Century,* New York, 1900.

Hefelbower, S. G., *The Relations of John Locke to English Deism,* Chicago, 1918.
Hertling, George Freiherr von, *John Locke und die Schule vom Cambridge,* Freiburg, 1892.
Hertz, Gerald Berkeley, *English Public Opinion after the Restoration,* London, 1902.
Hobbes, Thomas, *English Works.* Edited by William Molesworth, 11 vols., London, 1839-1845.
Thomae Hobbes Malmesburiensis opera philosophica quae latine scripsit . . . . Edited by William Molesworth, 5 vols., London, 1839-1845.
Hobhouse, Stephen, *William Law and Eighteenth Century Quakerism,* New York, 1928.
Hume, David, *Philosophical Works.* Edited by T. H. Green and T. H. Grose, 4 vols., London, 1882.
——, *Essays and Treatises on Several Subjects,* 2 vols., London, 1882.
Hunt, John, *History of Religious Thought in England,* 3 vols., London, 1870.
Inge, William Ralph, *The Platonic Tradition in English Religious Thought,* London, 1926.
King, Peter Lord, *The Life of John Locke, with extracts from his Correspondence, Journals and Common-place Books,* London, 1829.
Kittredge, George Lyman, *Witchcraft in Old and New England,* Cambridge (U.S.A.), 1929.
Lamprecht, Sterling Power, *The Moral and Political Philosophy of John Locke,* New York, 1918.
Lecky, W. E. H., *History of the Rise and Influence of the Spirit of Rationalism,* revised edition, 2 vols., New York, 1903.
Leland, John, *A View of the Principal Deistical Writers,* 2 vols., London, 1807.
Locke, John, *Works,* eleventh edition, 10 vols., London, 1812.
——, *An Essay Concerning the Human Understanding,* 2 vols., Oxford, 1894.
McGiffert, Arthur Cushman, *The Rise of Modern Religious Ideas,* New York, 1915.
McGlothlin, W. J., *Baptist Confessions of Faith,* Philadelphia, 1911.
Mallet, C. E., *A History of the University of Oxford,* Oxford, vols. ii and iii, 1924-1927.
Masson, David, *The Life of John Milton,* second edition, 6 vols., London, 1881.
Mayor, J. E. B., *Cambridge under Queen Anne,* Cambridge, 1911.
Mullinger, James Bass, *The University of Cambridge,* vol. iii, Cambridge, 1911.
Ornstein, Martha, *The Role of the Scientific Societies in the Seventeenth Century,* New York, 1913.

Notestein, Wallace, *A History of Witchcraft in England from 1558-1718,* Washington, 1911.
Pattison, Mark, "Tendencies of Religious Thought in England, 1688-1750," in *Essays and Reviews,* Oxford, 1889.
Phelps, William Lyon, *The Beginnings of the English Romantic Movement,* Boston, 1904.
Rand, Benjamin, *Life, Unpublished Letters and Philosophical Regimen of the Third Earl of Shaftesbury,* London and New York, 1900.
Rigaud, S. J., *Letters of Scientific Men of the Seventeenth Century,* 2 vols., Oxford, 1841.
Royce, Josiah, *The Spirit of Modern Philosophy,* Boston and New York, 1892.
Ritchie, David George, *Natural Rights,* third edition, London, 1916.
Rutherford, Samuel, *Letters.* Edited by Andrew A. Bonar, Edinburgh and London, n.d.
Seaton, A. A., *The Theory of Toleration under the later Stuarts,* Cambridge, 1911.
Seth, James, *English Philosophers and Schools of Philosophy,* London and New York, 1912.
Sedgwick, Henry, *Outlines of the History of Ethics,* fifth edition, London, 1910.
Third Earl of Shaftesbury, Anthony Ashley Cooper, *Characteristics, of Men, Manners, Opinions, Times, etc.* . . . Edited by J. M. Robertson, 2 vols., London, 1900.
Smith, Preserved, *The History of Modern Culture,* vol. i, New York, 1930.
Smyth, John, *The Works of John Smyth, Fellow of Christ's College, 1594-1598.* Tercentenary edition for the Baptist Historical Society with notes and bibliography by W. T. Whitley, 2 vols., Cambridge, 1915. [Important for ideas of Baptists in seventeenth century.]
Sorley, A. M., *A History of English Philosophy,* Cambridge, 1920.
Spingarn, J. E. [ed.], *Critical Essays of the Seventeenth Century,* 2 vols., Oxford, 1908.
Sprat, Thomas, *History of the Royal Society of London for the Improving of Natural Knowledge,* London, 1667.
Stephen, Leslie, *History of English Thought in the Eighteenth Century,* third edition, 2 vols., New York, 1902.
Stillingfleet, Edward, *Works.* Edited by Richard Bentley, 6 vols., London, 1709-1710.
Tillotson, John, *Works.* Edited by T. Birch, 12 vols., London, 1757.
Tindal, Matthew, *Christianity as Old as the Creation,* Newburgh, 1798 (first edition, London, 1730).
Toland, John, *Christianity not Mysterious,* London, 1702.
Tulloch, John, *Rational Theology and Christian Philosophy in England in the Seventeenth Century,* second edition, 2 vols., London, 1874.

Ward, Richard, *The Life of the Learned and Pious Dr. Henry More, late Fellow of Christ College in Cambridge. To which are annex'd Divers of his Useful and Excellent Letters*, London, 1710.
Warburton, William, *The Works of the Right Reverend William Warburton, D.D.*, 12 vols., London, 1811.
Whitehead, Alfred North, *Science and the Modern World*, New York, 1927 (Lowell Lectures, 1925).

IV. Sources for the Study of English Enthusiasm (c. 1640-c. 1740)[1]

[Allen, William], *The Danger of Enthusiasm Discovered, In An Epistle To The Quakers* .... London .... *1674* (McAlpin).
An Appeal from the Prophets to their Prophecies. Evidencing the new Dispensation they pretend, to be of the same stamp and authority with their Predictions. Which here are prov'd full of Falsity, by some notorious and undeniable Instances, that may be prov'd from Ear-Witnesses of unquestionable Credit, or other Authentick Record, when occasion serves, London .... *1708* (Aitken).
Annesley, Samuel [ed.], *A Continuation Of Morning-Exercise Questions and Cases of Conscience, Practically Resolved by Sundry Ministers* .... London .... *1683* (B. M.).
A[tterbury], F[rancis], *The Voice of the People, no Voice of God: or, The Mistaken Arguments of a Fiery Zealot, in a late Pamphlet Entitil'd Vox Populi, Vox Dei* .... *By F. A. D. D.* .... *1710* (B. M.).
Barclay, Robert, *The Anarchy Of The Ranters And Other Libertines, The Hierarchy of the Romanists, and other Pretended Churches, equally Refused and Refuted in a Two-fold Apology for the Church and People called in Derision Quakers* .... *1676* (B. M.).
——, *The Possibility & Necessity of the Inward and Immediate Revelation of the Spirit of God, Towards the Foundation and Ground of true Faith, Proved, In a Letter writ in Latin to the Herr Paets; And now also put into English* .... London, *1703* (B. M.).
——, *Apology for the True Christian Divinity*, Stereotype Edition, Philadelphia, 1908.
Bastwick, John, *The Second part of that Book call'd Independency Not Gods Ordinance: Or The Post-script, discovering the uncharitable dealing of the Independents towards their Christian brethren, with*

---

[1] The libraries in which scarce and rare items have been consulted are indicated as follows:

Aitken = Aitken Collection, University of Texas
B. M.   = British Museum
McAlpin = McAlpin Collection, Union Theological Seminary
Wrenn   = Wrenn Library, University of Texas.

the jugglings of many of their Pastors and Ministers .... London .... *1645* (McAlpin).

Bauthumley, Jacob, *The Light and Dark Sides of God or a plain and brief Discourse, of The light side God, Heaven and Earth. The dark side Devill, Sin, and Hell. As also of the Resurrection and Scripture. All which are set forth in their Severall Natures and Beings, according to the spirituality of the Scripture* .... London .... [1650] (B. M.).

Baxter, Richard, *The Certainty of the World Of Spirits. Fully evinced by unquestionable Histories of Apparitions and Witchcrafts, Operations, Voices, &c.* ... London .... *1691* (McAlpin).

———, *The Practical Works of Richard Baxter*, 4 vols., London, 1854.

Bisset, William, *The Modern Fanatick. With a Large and True Account of the Life, Actions, Endowments, &c. of the Famous Dr. Sa———l* .... London, 1710.

Blanc, John, *The Anathema of the False Prophets. In a Sermon Preach'd in several French Churches in and about London .... Now translated into English*, London, *1708* (Aitken).

Bugg, Francis, Sr., *The Picture Of Quakerism Drawn to the Life* .... London, ... *1697*.

Bulkeley, Sir Richard, *An Answer to Several Treatises Lately publish'd on the Subject of the Prophets. The first part*, London, *1708*.

Butler, Samuel, *Hudibras*. With annotations and preface by Zachary Grey, Cambridge, 1744.

Byron, John, "Enthusiasm: a poetical essay," in Chalmers, *The Works of the English Poets*, vol. xv, pp. 248-252.

Calamy, Edmund, *A Caveat against New Prophets* .... London, 1708.

Campbell, Archibald, *A Discourse proving that the Apostles were no Enthusiasts. Wherein the Nature and Influence of Religious Enthusiasm are impartially Explain'd* .... London, *1730*.

Casaubon, Meric, *A Treatise Concerning Enthusiasme, As it is an Effect of Nature: but is mistaken by many for either Divine Inspiration, or Diabolical Possession* .... London .... *1655*.

———, *A True & Faithful Relation of what passed for many Years Between Dr. John Dee (a Mathematician of great Fame in Q. Eliz. and King James their Reignes) and Some Spirits* .... *Out of The Original Copy, written with Dr. Dees own Hand: Kept in the Library of Sir. Tho. Cotton, Kt. Baronet, with a Preface Confirming the Reality (as to the Point of Spirits) of This Relation and shewing the several good Uses that a sober Christian may make of all. By Meric Casaubon, D.D.*, London .... *1659* (B. M.).

———, *Of Credulity and Incredulity; In things Divine & Spiritual: Wherein (among other things) A true and faithful account is given Of The Platonick Philosophy, As it hath reference to Christianity: As also the business of Witches and Witchcraft Against a late Writer, fully Argued and Disputed* . . . . London . . . . *1670* (McAlpin).

Chishull, Edmund, *The Great Danger and Mistake of all New Uninspir'd Prophecies, Relating to the End of the World. Being a Sermon Preach'd on Nov. 23d, 1707. At Serjeants-Inn-Chappel, in Chancery-Lane* . . . . London, 1708 (B. M.).

[Comber, Thomas], *Christianity No Enthusiasm: Or, The Several Kinds of Inspirations and Revelations Pretended to by the Quakers, Tried, and found Destructive To Holy Scripture and True Religion: In Answer to Thomas Ellwood's Defence thereof; in his Tract, Miscalled Truth Prevailing, &c.* . . . London . . . . *1678* (McAlpin).

A Confutation of the Prophets: Or, Mr. Lacy brought to a Right Understanding. By a Person of Honour [Pr. 119:105; 2 Peter 7:19], London . . . . 1708 (Aitken).

The Dangerous Imposture of Quakerism, represented in a Letter to a Friend; Or, a Brief Discourse concerning the True Nature and Pernicious Consequences of Canting about Religion . . . . London, *1699* (B. M.).

[Deacon, John], *The Grand Imposter Examined; Or, The Life, Tryal and Examination Of James Nayler, The Seduced and Seducing Quaker With the Manner of his Riding into Bristol* . . . . London . . . . *1656* (McAlpin).

Dell, William, *Several Sermons and Discourses of William Dell, Minister of the Gospel* . . . . London . . . . *1652.*

———, *The Stumbling-Stone, Or, A Discourse touching that offence which the World and Worldly Church do take against 1. Christ Himself. 2. His true Word. 3. His true Worship. 4. His true Church. 5. His true Government. 6. His true Ministry* . . . . London . . . . *1653.*

———, *The Tryall of Spirits Both in Teachers & Hearers. Wherein is held forth The clear Discovery, and certain Downfal Of The Carnal and Antichristian Clergie of These Nations. Testified from the Word of God to the University-Congregation in Cambridge* . . . . *Whereunto is added A plain and necessary Confutation of divers Errors Delivered By Mr. Sydrach Simpson In a Sermon preached to the same Congregation the last Commencement there, Anno 1653* . . . . *With a brief Testimony against Divinity-Degrees in the Universities. As also, Luther's Testimony at large upon the whole matter. And lastly, The right Reformation of Learning, Schools, and Universities, according to the state of the Gospel, and the light that shines therein* . . . . London . . . . *1653.*

[In my own copy of Dell's sermons, *A Plain and Necessary Confutation* . . . . has a separate title-page, dated 1654, and is separately paged. The *Testimony Against Divinity Degrees, Luther's Testimony* and *Right Reformation* are paged together.]

A Description of the Sect called the Familie of Love: with their common place of residence. Being discovered by one Mrs. Susanna Snow of Pirford near Chersey in the County of Surrey, who was vainly led away for a time through their base allurement, and at length fell mad, till by a great miracle shewn from God, she was delivered . . . . London printed, 1641 (B. M.).

A Discovery Of 29. Sects here in London, all of which, except the first, are most Divelish and Damnable . . . Printed Anno, 1641 (McAlpin).

D'Urfey, Thomas, *The Modern Prophets: Or, New Wit for a Husband. A Comedy. As it is Acted at the Theatre-Royal in Drury-Lane, By Her Majesty's Servants* . . . . London, 1709 (Wrenn).

Edwards, Thomas, *Gangraena: Or A Catalogue and Discovery of many of the Errours, Heresies, Blasphemies and pernicious Practices of the Sectaries of this time, vented and acted in England in these four last years: As Also, A Particular Narration of divers Stories, Remarkable Passages, Letters; an Extract of many Letters, all concerning the present Sects; together with some Observations upon, and Corollaries from all the fore-named Premises* . . . . London . . . . 1646 [1645?] (McAlpin).

———, *The Second Part Of Gangraena: Or a fresh and further Discovery of the Errors, Heresies, Blasphemies, and dangerous Proceedings of the Sectaries of this time* . . . . *A Reply to the most materiall exceptions made by Mr. Saltmarsh, Mr. Walwyn, and Cretensis, against Mr. Edwards late Book entituled Gangraena. As also brief Animadversions upon some late Pamphlets; one of Mr. Bacons, another of Thomas Webs, a third of a Picture made in disgrace of the Presbyterians* . . . . London . . . . 1646 (McAlpin).

———, *The Third Part of Gangraena: Or, A new and higher Discovery of the Errors, Heresies, Blasphemies, and insolent Proceedings of the Sectaries of these times* . . . . *Briefe Animadversions on many of the Sectaries late Pamphlets, as Lilburnes and Overtons Books against the House of Peeres. M. Peters his last Report of the English Warres, The Lord Mayors Farewell from his Office of Maioralty, M. Goodwins thirty-eight Queres upon the Ordinance against Heresies and Blasphemies, M. Burtons Conformities Deformity, M. Dells Sermon before the House of Commons* . . . . *As also some few Hints and briefe observations on divers Pamphlets written lately against me and some of my Books, as M. Goodwins pretended Reply to the Antapologie, M. Burroughs Vindication, Lanseters Lance, Gangrena playes Rex, Gangraena-Chrestum, M. Saltmarshes Answer to the second part of Gangraena* . . . London . . . 1646 (McAlpin).

[Etherington, J.], *A Brief Discovery Of The Blasphemous Doctrine of Familisme, First conceived and brought forth into the world by one Henry Nicolas of the Low Countries of Germany about one hundred years agoe; And now very boldly taught by one Mr. Randall, and sundry others in and about the Citie of London* .... London .... *1645* (McAlpin).

Featley, Daniel, Καταβάπτισται κατάπτυστοι. *The Dippers dipt; Or The Anabaptists Duck'd and Plung'd over Head and Eares, at a Disputation in Southwark* .... London .... 1645 [1644?] (McAlpin).

Fisher, Samuel, Παιδοβαπτίζοντες Παιδίζοντες. *Baby-Baptism Meer Babism. Or An Answer To No-Body in five words to Every-Body who finds himself concern'd in it. I. Anti-Diabolism .... II. Anti-Babism .... III. Anti-Rantism .... IV. Anti-Ranterism* .... London .... *1653* (McAlpin).

Fox, George, *The Journal of George Fox.* Revised Text edited by Norman Penney, F.S.A., London, 1924.

——, *The Journal of George Fox.* Edited from the MSS. by Norman Penney, F.S.A., with an Introduction by Edmund Harvey, M.A., 2 vols., Cambridge, 1911. *Works,* 8 vols., Philadelphia and New York.

Glanvill, Joseph, *Philosophia Pia; Or, A Discourse Of The Religious Temper, and Tendencies Of The Experimental Philosophy, Which is profest By the Royal Society. To which is annext A Recommendation, and Defence of Reason in the Affairs of Religion* .... London .... *1671* (McAlpin).

——, *Essays On Several Important Subjects In Philosophy And Religion* .... London .... *1676* (McAlpin).

——, *Saducismus Triumphatus: Or, Full and Plain Evidence Concerning Witches And Apparitions .... With a Letter of Doctor Henry More on the Same Subject* .... London .... *1681* (McAlpin).

Graunt, John, *Truths Victory Against Heresie; All sorts comprehended under these ten mentioned* .... London .... *1645* (McAlpin).

Hickes, George, *The Spirit of Enthusiasm Exorcised, In A Sermon Preached Before this University Of Oxford, on Act-Sunday, July 11, 1680* ..... London .... 1680 (McAlpin).

[Hoadly, Benjamin], *A Brief Vindication of the Antient Prophets from the Imputation and Misrepresentations of such as adhere to our Present Pretenders to Inspiration. In a Letter to Sir Richard Bulkeley, Bart* .... London, 1709 (B. M.).

Hobbes, Thomas, *Leviathan Or The Matter, Forme and Power Of A Commonwealth Ecclesiasticall And Civill. By Thomas Hobbes of Malmesbury. London Printed for Andrew Crooke, at the Green Dragon in St. Paul's Church-yard, 1651* (Wrenn).

Holland, John, *The Smoke Of The Bottomlesse Pit: Or, A More true and fuller Discovery of the Doctrine of those men which call themselves Ranters: Or, The Mad Crew* .... London .... *1651* (McAlpin).

The Honest Quaker: or, the Forgeries and Impostures of the Pretended French Prophets and their Abettors Expos'd; In a Letter From a Quaker to his Friend, giving an account of a Show-Miracle Perform'd by John L—y Esq.; on the Body of Elizabeth Gray, on the 17th of August last, London, 1707 (Aitken).

How, Samuel, *The Sufficiencie Of The Spirits Teaching, Without Humane-Learning: Or, A Treatise, Tending to Prove Humane-Learning To Be No Help To the Spiritual understanding of the Word of God . . . . Seen, Allowed, and Printed, by us . . . .* 1640 (McAlpin).

Hutchinson, Francis (Minister of Bury St. Edwards in Suffolk), *A Short View of the Pretended Spirit of Prophecy, Taken from its First Rise in the Year 1688, to its Present State among us. Together with some Observations upon their Doctrines and pretended Miracles. And Examples of such like Delusions in the world . . . .* London, 1708 (Aitkin).

[Jackson, John], *A Sober Word To A Serious People: Or, A Moderate Discourse Respecting As well The Seekers (so called) As The Present Churches . . . .* London . . . . 1651 (McAlpin).

Keith, George, *Immediate Revelation, (Or, Jesus Christ The Eternal Son of God, Revealed in Man, Revealing the Knowledge of God, and the things of his Kingdom, Immediately) Not Ceased, But Remaining a standing and perpetual Ordinance in the Church of Christ . . . . The Second Edition . . . .* 1676 (McAlpin).

[Kingston, Richard], *Enthusiastick Impostors no Divinely Inspired Prophets. Being an Historical Relation of the Rise, Progress, and present Practices of the French and English Pretended Prophets . . . .* London, 1707 (B. M.).

Lacy, John, *A Relation of the Dealings of God to his unworthy servant John Lacy, since the time of his believing and professing himself inspir'd.* London, 1708 (B. M.).

———, *Mr. Lacy's Letter to the Reverend Josiah Woodward, concerning his remarks on the Modern Prophets,* London, 1708 (B. M.).

———, *A Cry from the Desart: or, Testimonials of the Miraculous Things Lately come to pass in the Cevennes, Verified upon Oath, and by other Proofs. Translated from the Originals. The Second Edition . . . .* London, 1707 (B. M.).

[Lacy wrote a preface to this edition. There is no indication as to the translator.]

Leo, William, *A Sermon Preached at Lambeth, April 21, 1645, at the Funerall Of that Learned and Polemicall Divine, Daniel Featley, Doctor in Divinity, Late Preacher there. With a short Relation of his Life and Death . . . .* London . . . . 1645 (B. M.).

[Marion, Elias], *The French Prophet's Declaration; or, an Account of* the Preachings, Prophecies and Warnings of Elias Marion, One of the Chief of the pretended Inspir'd Protestant Prophets and others of them . . . . Translated from the Original, taken from his own Mouth in Writing . . . . London, 1707 (B. M.).

Milton, John, *Johannis Miltoni Angli de Doctrina Christiana libri duo posthumi* . . . . Cambridge, 1825.

[Ministers of London], *The humble Petition of the Ministers of the City of London* . . . . London . . . . *1644* (B. M.).

[Ministers of Yorkshire], *Vindiciae Veritatis Or an Unanimous Attestation to God's blessed Truth Revealed in his Word: Together with a serious Protestation against those Church-desolating and Soul-damning Errors, Heresies, and Blasphemies, which of late have come in like a flood upon our County and Kingdome: Especially against a Toleration of them. Made in pursuance of the National Covenant, By The Ministers of the Gospel within the West-Riding of the Countie of York* . . . . London . . . . *1648* [signed by forty-one ministers] (McAlpin).

More, Henry, *Enthusiasmus Triumphatus, Or, A Discourse Of The Nature, Causes, Kinds, and Cure, of Enthusiasme; Written by Philophilus Parresiastes, and prefixed to Alazononomastix His Observations and Reply: Whereunto is added a Letter of his to a private Friend, wherein certain passages in his Reply are vindicated and severall matters relating to Enthusiasme more fully cleared*. . . . London . . . . *1656* (McAlpin).

——, *A Collection Of Several Philosophical Writings Of Dr. Henry More*. The second edition, London, *1662* (contains *Enthusiasmus Triumphatus*).

Muggleton, Lodowick, *The Acts of the Witnesses Of The Spirit. In Five Parts. By Lodowick Muggleton: One of the Two Witnesses, and True Prophets of the only High, Immortal, Glorious God, Christ Jesus. Left by him to be publish'd after's death* . . . . London . . . *1699* (McAlpin). [The McAlpin collection contains several Muggletonian tracts].

Nicholson, Henry, *The Falshood of the New Prophets Manifested with their Corrupt Doctrines and Conversations. By one who hath had intimate Conversation with them, whilst he had an Opinion of their Integrity: But now thinks himself obliged to discover their Enormities, for the Publick Benefit* . . . . London, 1708 (B. M.).

N[iclas], H[endrik], *An Introduction To The holy Understanding of the Glasse of Righteousnesse. Wherein are uttered many notable admonitions and exhortations to the good Life* . . . . London . . . . *1649* (McAlpin)

Pagitt, Ephraim, *Heresiography: Or, A description of the Hereticks and Sectaries of these latter times* . . . . London . . . . *1645* (McAlpin).

Penn, William, *Select Works*, 5 vols., London, 1782.

The Ranters Creed. Being a true copie of the Examinations of a blasphemous sort of people, commonly called Ranters. Whose Names are herein particularised, together with the name of their pretended god almighty, and their false Prophet. Taken before Thomas Hubbert Esquire, one of the Justices of the Peace for the County of Middlesex . . . . London . . . . 1651 (McAlpin).

The Ranting of the Ranters. Being a full Relation of their uncivil carriages, and blasphemous words and actions at their mad meetings, their several kind of musick, dances, and ryatings, and their belief and opinions concerning heaven and hell . . . . [1650, B. M., this will illustrate a large number of pamphlets of little or no historical value except as reflections of public excitement. Typical titles are: *The Ranters Religion . . . . 1650* (McAlpin), *A Looking-Glass For The Ranters . . . . 1653* (McAlpin), *The Arraignment and Tryall with a Declaration of the Ranters . . . . 1650* (B. M.)].

Reflections on Sir Richard Bulkeley's Answer to Several Treatises, lately publish'd on the Subject of the Prophets . . . . London, 1708 (B. M.).

A Reply to the Main Argument in a Paper Entitled, An Impartial Account of the Prophets, In a Letter to a Friend, London, 1708.

Rutherford, Samuel, *A Survey Of The Spirituall Antichrist. Opening The Secrets of Familisme and Antinomianisme in the Antichristian Doctrine of John Saltmarsh, and Will. Del, the present Preachers of the Army now in England, and of Robert Town, Tot Crisp, H. Denne, Eaton, and others. In which is revealed the rise and spring of Antinomians, Familists, Libertines, Swenck-feldians Enthysiasts, &c. . . . London . . . . 1648* (McAlpin).

Salmon, Joseph, *Heights in Depts And Depts in Heights. Or Truth no less Secretly then Sweetly sparkling out its Glory from under a Cloud of Obloquie . . . . London . . . . 1651* (B. M.).

Sedgwick, Joseph, *A Sermon, Preached at St. Marie's in the University of Cambridge May 1st, 1653. Or, An Essay to the discovery of the Spirit of Enthusiasme and pretended Inspiration, that disturbs and strikes at the Universities: . . . Together with An Appendix, wherein Mr. Del's Stumbling-stone is briefly repli'd unto: And A fuller discourse of the use of Universities and Learning upon an Ecclesiasticall account, submitted by the same Authour to the judgement of every impartial and rational Christian . . . London . . . 1653* (McAlpin).

Smith, John, *Select Discourses . . . . London . . . . 1660* [the first discourse treats "Of a true Way or Method of Attaining to Divine Knowledge" and the sixth "Of Prophecy"].

South, Robert, "Enthusiasts not led by the Spirit of God" (two sermons in *Sermons*, new edition, 5 vols., Oxford, 1842).

Spinckes, Thomas, *The New Pretenders to Prophecy re-examined* . . . . London, 1710.

Take warning before it be too late: Or, Notice to the City of London, By way of advice, to take heed of Sectaries, and dangerous proceedings, very likely to befall her . . . . *By a Friend who very well understands the great danger the City at this present is in* . . . . *Printed in the Yeare, 1648* (B. M.).

Taylor, John, *A Swarme Of Sectaries, And Schismatiques: Wherein is discovered the strange preaching (or prating) of such as are by their trades Coblers, Tinkers, Pedlers, Weavers, Sow-gelders, and Chymney-Sweepers* . . . . *Printed luckily, and may be read unhappily, betwixt hawke and buzzard, 1641* (McAlpin).

Underhill, E. B. [ed.], *Tracts on Liberty of Conscience and Persecution, 1614-1661*, London, 1846 (Hanserd Knollys Society Publications).

A Vindication of Learning From unjust Aspersions. Wherein Is set forth, the Learning of the Ancient Fathers, and Patriarches, Prophets and Apostles of Jesus Christ. And, Shewing how farre Learning is necessary to the true understanding, knowledge, and Preaching of the Gospel . . . . *London* . . . . *1646* (B. M.).

[Wharton, Henry], *The Enthusiasm Of The Church of Rome Demonstrated in some Observations upon the Life Of Ignatius Loyola, London* . . . . *1688* (McAlpin).

Woodward, Josiah, *Remarks on the Modern Prophets. And on some Arguments Lately Published in their Defence* . . . . London . . . . 1708 (Aitken).

——, *An Answer to the Letter of John Lacy, Esq.; Dated July 6, 1708, and Directed to Josiah Woodward, D.D.,* . . . . London, 1708.

——, *The copy of a Letter to Mr. F—. M—. A gentleman, who is a Follower of the Pretended Prophets. Shewing The Reasons why they ought to be accounted Impostors* [signed J. W.], London, 1708 (Aitken. In the Aitken Collection there is a volume of eleven tracts on the French Prophets which seem to have been collected by Woodward).

Whitfeld, William, *A Discourse Of Enthusiasm, Deliver'd in a Visitation-Sermon, At Guilford On Wednesday in Whitson-Week* . . . . *London* . . . . *1698* (McAlpin).

V. METHODISM AND METHODIST ENTHUSIASM

Bangs, Nathan, *Life of the Rev. Freeborn Garretson,* New York, 1829.
Benham, Daniel, *Memoirs of James Hutton,* London, 1886.
Bowman, William, *The Imposture of Methodism displayed,* London, 1740.
Coke, Thomas and Moore, Henry, *The Life of the Rev. John Wesley, A.M.,* . . . The First American Edition . . . . Philadelphia, 1793.

[1] [Cavender, Curtis H.], *Catalogue of Works in Refutation of Methodism, From its Origin in 1729 to the Present Time* .... Compiled by H. C. Decanver, Philadelphia, 1846.

Eayrs, George, *John Wesley: Christian Philosopher and Church Founder*, London, 1926.

Evans, Theophilus, *The History of Modern Enthusiasm, from the Reformation to the present time* ... The second edition ... London, 1757.

Gibson, Edmund, *The Bishop of London's Pastoral Letter to the People of his Diocese, Especially those of the two great cities of London and Westminster: By way of caution, Against Lukewarmness on one hand, and Enthusiasm on the other.* The second edition, London, 1739.

Green, Richard, *Anti-Methodist Publications*, London, 1902.

——, *Bibliography of the Works of John and Charles Wesley*. Second edition, London, 1906.

Green, Thomas, *A Dissertation on Enthusiasm*, London, 1758.

Hampson, John, *Memoirs of the late John Wesley*, Sunderland, 1791.

Hutton, W. H., *John Wesley*, London, 1927.

Lavington, George, Bishop of Exeter, *The Enthusiasm of Methodists and Papists compar'd* .... Three Parts .... London, 1749-51.

Lee, Umphrey, *The Lord's Horseman: a book about John Wesley*, New York, 1928.

Mason, A. J., *John Wesley. A Lecture*, London, 1908.

Mason, William, *Methodism displayed, and Enthusiasm detected.* The fifth edition, London, 1761.

Moore, Henry, *The Life of the Rev. John Wesley*, 2 vols., New York, 1824-25.

Nagler, Arthur Wilford, *Pietism and Methodism*, Nashville, 1918.

Nightingale, Joseph, *A Portraiture of Methodism: being an impartial view of the rise, progress, doctrines, discipline, and manners of the Wesleyan Methodists* .... London, 1807.

Osborn, George, *Outlines of Wesleyan Bibliography*, London, 1869.

Piette, Maximin, *La Réaction wesléyenne dans l'évolution protestante*, Brussels, 1925.

Scott, John, *A Fine Picture of Enthusiasm, chiefly drawn by Dr. John Scott, formerly rector of St. Gile's in the Fields* .... To which is added, an Application of the subject to the modern Methodists .... London, 1744.

Smalbroke, Richard, Bishop of Lichfield and Coventry, *A Charge to the Clergy of the Diocese of Lichfield and Coventry*, London, 1746.

Southey, Robert, *The Life of Wesley and the Rise and Progress of Methodism*, 2 vols., London, 1820.

[1] Cavender's collection of anti-Methodist publications is now in the library of the General Theological Seminary, New York.

BIBLIOGRAPHY

Taylor, Isaac, *Wesley and Methodism,* New York, 1852.
Telford, John, *Life of John Wesley,* London, 1900.
Townsend, W. J., Workman, H. B., Eayrs, George [eds.], *New History of Methodism,* 2 vols., London, 1909.
Trapp, Joseph, *The Nature, Folly, Sin and Danger of being Righteous over-much; with a particular View to the Doctrines and Practices of certain Modern Enthusiasts* . . . . London, 1739.
Tyerman, Luke, *Life and Times of Samuel Wesley the Elder,* London, 1866.
——, *Life and Times of John Wesley,* 3 vols., London, 1870.
——, *The Oxford Methodists,* London, 1873.
——, *Life of George Whitefield,* London, 1876.
Warburton, William, *The Doctrine of Grace: or, the Office and Operations of the Holy Spirit Vindicated from the Insults of Infidelity, and the Abuses of Fanaticism:* . . . In Three Books . . . . The second edition . . . . London, 1763.
Watkins-Jones, Howard, *The Holy Spirit from Arminius to Wesley,* London, 1929.
Watson, Richard, *The Life of the Rev. John Wesley, A.M.,* . . . First American Official Edition, with translations and notes by John Emory, New York, 1831.
Wesley, Charles, *Journal.* Edited by Thomas Jackson, London, 1849.
——, *The Journal of the Rev. Charles Wesley. The Early Journal,* London, n.d. (preface dated 1909).
Wesley Historical Society, *Proceedings,* Burnley, 1898-
Wesley, John, *The Journal of John Wesley.* Standard edition. Edited by Nehemiah Curnock, London, 1909-16.
——, *Letters of John Wesley.* Edited by George Eayrs, London, 1915.
——, *The Works of the Rev. John Wesley, A.M.,* 14 vols., London, 1872 [reprint of Jackson edition of 1831].
Wesley's Veterans: Lives of Early Methodist Preachers Told by Themselves, 7 vols., London, n.d.
Whitefield, George, *A Select Collection of Letters of the Late Reverend George Whitefield, M.A.,* . . . *From the year 1734 to 1770* . . . . In three volumes, London, 1772.
Workman, Herbert B., *Methodism,* Cambridge, 1912.
——, *The Place of Methodism in the Catholic Church.* New Edition, revised and enlarged, London, 1921. [This is substantially the same as chapter I in *New History of Methodism,* vol. i.]

VI. SOME MODERN WORKS ON MYSTICISM, ENTHUSIASM AND RELATED TOPICS

Crofts, J. E. V., "Enthusiasm," in *Eighteenth Century Literature. An Oxford Miscellany,* Oxford, 1909.

BIBLIOGRAPHY

Davenport, F. M., *Primitive Traits in Religious Revivals*, New York, 1905.

Delacroix, Henri, *Études d'histoire et de psychologie du mysticisme*, Paris, 1908.

Dimond, Sidney, *The Psychology of the Methodist Revival*, London, 1926.

Eynard, Samuel, *L'Enthousiasme*. Tours, 1894 (Thesis, Faculty of Protestant Theology in Paris).

Fleming, W. H., *Mysticism in Christianity*, London, 1913.

Gwatkin, Henry Melvill, *The Knowledge of God and its Historical Development*. Second edition, 2 vols., Edinburgh, 1908.

Hart, Bernard, *The Psychology of Insanity*, Cambridge, 1922.

Heim, Karl, *Das Gewissheitsproblem in der systematischen Theologie bis zu Schleiermacher*, Leipzig, 1911.

Herrmann, Willibald, *The Communion of the Christian with God*. Translated by J. Sandys Stanton, London, 1896.

Hügel, Baron Friederich von, *The Mystical Element of Religion*. Second edition, 2 vols., London and New York, 1922.

Inge, William Ralph, *Christian Mysticism*, New York, 1899.

——, *Faith and its Psychology*, New York, 1915.

James, William, *Varieties of Religious Experience*, London, 1915.

Leuba, James Henry, *The Psycholoyy of Religious Mysticism*, London and New York, 1925.

Knight, Rachel, *The Founder of Quakerism, A Psychological Study of the Mysticism of George Fox*, London, 1922.

Maréchal, Joseph, *Études sur la psychologie des mystiques*, tome i, Bruges et Paris, 1924 (Museum Lessianum Publications dirigées par des Pères de la Compagnie de Jésus, Louvain, Section Philosophique).

Montague, William Pepperrell, *Ways of Knowing*, London, 1925.

Morgan, John B., *The Psychology of Abnormal People*, New York, 1928.

Myerson, Abraham, *The Psychology of Mental Disorders*, New York, 1924.

Oesterreich, T. K., *Possession, Demoniacal and Other*, New York, 1930.

Poulain, Aug., *The Graces of Interior Prayer. A Treatise on Mystical Theology*. Translated from the sixth edition by Leonora L. Yorke Smith, London, n.d. (The English imprimatur is dated 1910.)

Radermacher, Ludwig, "Enthusiasm," in *Encyclopedia of Religion and Ethics*.

Royce, Josiah, "George Fox as a Mystic," *Harvard Theological Review*, 1913.

Taylor, Isaac, *Natural History of Enthusiasm*, London, 1829.

Thouless, Robert H., *An Introduction to the Psychology of Religion*, Cambridge, 1923.

Underhill, Evelyn, *Mysticism*, London, 1911.

——, *The Mystic Way*, London, 1913.

INDEX

Addison, Joseph, 115
America, Wesleys in, 123
Anabaptists, 34-35, 39
Annesley, Samuel, 110
Anthony of Padua, 131
Apostles, and enthusiasm, 19
Aquinas, St. Thomas, 27-28, 60
Aristotle, 67
Arminian Baptists, *vide* Baptists
Articles, the Forty-two, 38; the Thirty-nine, 38
Atterbury, Francis, bishop of Rochester, 106
Augsburg Confession, 38
Authority, ecclesiastical, 24, 34, 64-65, 73-75, 144; seat of religious, 23-24, 35, 39, 41-42, 49, 50-51, 58, 62-64, 68-69, 75
Averroes, 26

Bacchus, *vide* Dionysos
Bacon, Francis, 76-77
Balaam, 17
Baptists, 39-43, 50, 103, 105
Barclay, Robert, 62-63, 74, 75, 91
Bastwick, John, 47
Bauthumley, Jacob, 54
Baxter, Richard, 49, 53-54, 62, 64, 108, 110
Benedict XIV, 30
Blackburne, Francis, 130
Blair, Robert, 123
Boehme, Jacob, 43, 53, 139
Boyle, Robert, 76
Browne, Sir Thomas, 76
Brownists, 48
Buckingham, Duchess of, 129
Bulkeley, Sir Richard, 56, 57, 100, 104, 110
Burnet, Gilbert, bishop of Salisbury, 38, 108-109
Butler, Samuel, 107

Cajetan, Cardinal, 28-29
Calamy, Edmund, 64-65, 71
Calvert, Giles, 105

Calvin, John, 34-36, 65
Calvinistic Baptists, *vide* Baptists
Calvinists, 107
Cambridge Platonists, 75, 84, 87, 98; *vide* Glanvill, More, John Smith, Whichcote
Canon Law, on immediate inspiration, 26-27
Carlstadt, Andrew Bodenstein of, 32
Casaubon, Isaac, 77
Casaubon, Meric, 77-80, 89, 95, 109
Catherine of Siena, 131
Catholic, *vide* Roman Catholic
Cennick, John, 126, 127
Cevennes, prophets of, 56
Charismata, *vide* Gifts of the Spirit
Church of England, 38, 42, 44, 65, 102, 112
Church, Thomas, 143
Cicero, 13, 76, 95
Clarendon Code, 99
Comber, Thomas, 58-59, 104, 105
Conversion, 132-133, 140-141
Corybantes, 14
Courthope, W. J., 117
Cromwell, Oliver, 46, 77, 78

David, 19
Decorum, eighteenth-century, 112-115
Dee, John, 104n
Deism, 68-70, 75
Dell, William, 43, 67-68
Democracy, connection with enthusiasm, 104-107
Dennis, John, 113, 116
Didache, 22
Diggers, The, 104, 105
Dionysos, cult of, 13-14
Dissent, 65, 108, 112; *vide* also Independents, Presbyterians
Divination, Augustine on, 25; Francis Bacon on, 76-77; Peucer on, 36-37; Roman, 17
Dominic, St., 131

173

Dryden, John, 107
Dunton, John, 110
D'Urfey, Thomas, 116

Ecstasy, Benedict XIV on, 30; Dionysiac, 14; of French Prophets, 57, 99-100, 111; Montanist, 23-24; in New Testament, 19; in Old Testament, 17; Philonic, 18; Platonic, 15
Edict of Nantes, Revocation of, 56
Edwards, Thomas, 44, 102
Enthusiasm, definition of: Casaubon's, 78; Cicero's, 13; Lavington's, 131; Locke's, 93; Shaftesbury's, 96; Wesley's, 138; distinguished from mysticism, 16; meaning in 17th century, 58; in 18th century, 96, 116; origin of word, 13
Episcopalians, *vide* Church of England
Etherington, J., 49
Euripides, 13-14
Eusebius of Caesarea, 23
Evans, Theophilus, 124-125, 127-128, 135
Exorcism, 22, 57
Experience, religious, Luther on, 33; Wesley on, 124, 141-142, 147-148

Faith, 28, 34, 69, 70, 81-82, 93, 139-141
Familists, *vide* Family of Love
Family of Love, 48-50
Featley, Daniel, 39-40
Fifth Monarchy Men, 43, 103, 105-106
Forty-two Articles, 38
Fox, George, 50-51, 71-72, 73, 99, 100-101, 105
Francis, St., 131
French Prophets, 56-57, 71, 99-100, 104, 110-111, 122, 141
Friends, Society of, *vide* Quakers
Furly, Benjamin, 90-91

General Baptists, *vide* Baptists
Gerson, John, 29-30
Gibson, Edmund, bishop of London, 131-133, 135
Gifts of the Spirit, Thomas Aquinas on, 28; Baptists on, 40-42; in early church, 21-22, 24; Gibson on, 132; Hickes on, 60; Paul on, 20-21; Sedgwick on, 67; Warburton on, 70-71; Wesley on, 136
Glanvill, Joseph, 68, 87-89, 109
Goodwin, Thomas, 104n
Grace, 27-28, 60, 70-71, 139
Greeks, enthusiasm among, 13-16
Green, Matthew, 114

Hanotaux, Gabriel, 31
Harnack, A., 23
Herbert, George, 143
Hebrews, prophecy of, 17
Hickes, George, 60
High Church, 75, 76, 129-130
Hildegard, St., 25n
Hobbes, Thomas, 80-84, 89, 110
Holland, John, 54-55
Holy Club, 120-121
Holy Spirit, in *Acts of the Apostles*, 19; Baptists on, 40-42; Barclay on, 63; Baxter on, 64; Calvin on, 35-36; Comber on, 59; in early church, 22-24; Luther on, 34, 36; Milton on, 63-64; in Old Testament, 17; in Pauline letters, 19-21; Rutherford on, 64; Sedgwick on, 67; Zwickau prophets on, 34; *vide* also Witness of the Spirit
Hortatory Address to the Greeks, 22
How, Samuel, 65-66, 102
Human nature, theories of, 15-16, 72, 75, 139
Hume, David, 102, 107
Huntingdon, Selina, Countess of, 129

Independents, 44
Infallibility, 72, 75, 96-97, 108-109, 147
Innate ideas, 68, 89, 139
Inner light, 50-51
Insanity, *vide* Madness
Inspiration, of Hebrew prophets, 17-18; Philonic theory of, 17-18; Platonic theory of, 14; of Scripture, *vide* Scriptures
Irenaeus, 22

Jessop, Augustus, 109
Jesus Christ, 19
Joachim of Fiore, 25
Joan of Arc, 31

INDEX

John of Rupescissa, 25-26
Justin Martyr, 21-22

King, Peter, first Baron King of Ockham, 144

Lacy, John, 56, 57, 104
Latitudinarians, 68, 75
Lavington, George, bishop of Exeter, 122, 130-131
Law, William, 139
Lay preaching, 26, 102-103, 127-128, 135
Lecky, W. E. H., 89, 98, 109, 135
Leslie, Charles, 115
Levellers, 104-105, 106
Lilburne, John, 44
Literature, English, and enthusiasm, 112-113, 116-118
Locke, John, 76, 89-95, 110, 139
Love, and inspiration, 14
Lower classes, and enthusiasm, 102-104
Loyola, St. Ignatius, 108, 131
Luther, Martin, 31-34, 60, 65, 124

Madness, 14-15, 18, 98-99, 99-102
Marion, Elias, 110-111
Martyr, Justin, *vide* Justin
Medical theories of enthusiasm, 79, 86-87, 110
Melanchthon, 32, 36, 38
Mennonites, 39
Methodists, origins of, 120; preaching of, 124-125; 127-128, 135; singing of, 125; scenes at early meetings, 124-127, 136-137; social class of, 127-128; *vide* also Wesley, John
Middleton, Conyers, 141
Milton, John, 63-64
Ministry, calling of, 26, 34, 65, 135, 144-145; controversy over learned, 65-68
Molyneux, Thomas, 91-92
Montanism, 23-24, 65
More, Henry, 84-87, 89, 95, 110
Muggleton, Lodowick, 55-56
Mysticism, and enthusiasm, distinguished, 16; and individualism, 71-72

Natural religion, 69-70
Nayler, James, 51-52
Neo-Platonism, 17; *vide* Plotinus

Newton, Isaac, 76
Niclas, Hendrick, 48-49
Nye, Philip, 104n

Oglethorpe, General James Edward, 123
Oracles, 13, 80
Ordination, Wesley on, 144-145
Original sin, and enthusiasm, 72
Owen, John, 104n

Paets, Adrian, 91
Pagitt, Ephraim, 48-49
Pantheism, of Ranters, 54
Paraclete, 23
Particular Baptists, *vide* Baptists
Paul, St., 19-21, 22, 55
Penington, Isaac, 53
Penn, William, 56, 73, 105
Pentecost, 19, 21
Pepys, Samuel, 102
Peucer, Caspar, 36-37
Philo Judaeus, 17-17, 22
Philosophy, and inspiration, 15; *vide* Aquinas, Bacon, Hobbes, Locke, Shaftesbury
Plato, 14-16
Plotinus, 16
Poetry, and inspiration, 14-15; *vide* Romantic Movement
Politics, and enthusiasm, 111-112
Preaching, *vide* Lay preaching, Methodists, Ministry
Presbyterians, 43, 75, 107; *vide* Baxter, Edwards, Rutherford, Westminster Confession
Private revelation, *vide* Revelation
Prophecy, Thomas Aquinas on, 28; Benedict XIV on, 30; Dionysiac, 14; in early church, 20, 21-24; Hebrew, 17; Hobbes on, 83-84; mediaeval, 25-26; Montanist, 23-24; Platonic, 14; in 17th century, 109; John Smyth on, 61-62; Warburton on, 70
Psychology, of enthusiasm, 94-95, 96, 100
Puritans, 48, 107, 109

Quakers, 42, 44, 50-53, 72-75, 101-102, 108; and Fifth Monarchy, Men, 106; and Levellers, 104-105; social class of, 103-104; theology of, 52-53

INDEX

Randall, a Familist, 49-50
Ranters, 42, 53-55, 105
Rationalism, in 17th and 18th centuries, 109-111, 112
Revelation, deists on, 69-70; Hobbes on, 83-84; Locke on, 92-93; private revelation in Catholic doctrine, 29, 31; Rutherford on, 59-60; Wesley on private, 143
Robins, John, 55
Roman Catholics, enthusiasm associated with, 107-109, 129-131; *vide* Authority, Benedict XIV, Grace, Revelation, Witness of the Spirit
Romantic Movement in Literature, 116-118
Rosicrucians, 53
Royal Society, 68, 76, 88
Rutherford, Samuel, 48, 59, 64

Sacheverell, Henry, 115
Salmon, Joseph, 54
Saul, 17
Schmalkaldic Articles, 34
Science, experimental, 76, 88, 112
Scriptures, Baptists on, 40-43; Barclay on, 63-64; Baxter on, 62; Calvin on, 35-36; Church of England doctrine of, 38; Familist teaching on, 49-50; Fox on, 51; Luther on, 34, 36; Milton on, 63-64; Ranters on, 54; Presbyterian doctrine of, 39; Sedgwick on, 67; Rutherford on, 64; Wesley on, 143
Sectaries, 44-55
Seekers, 47, 50
Sedgwick, Joseph, 67-68
Semites, *vide* Hebrews
Shaftesbury, Anthony Ashley Cooper, third Earl of, 95-96, 114, 115, 116
Shepherd of Hermas, 22
Smallbrook, Richard, bishop of Lichfield and Coventry, 133
Smith, John, Cambridge Platonist, 61
Smith, John, the se-Baptist, *vide* Smyth

Smyth, John, 40-41, 42
Spirit, *vide* Holy Spirit
Stephen, bishop of Paris, 26
Stoics, 16
Swift, Jonathan, 100, 112

Tannye, Thomas (John), 55
Tertullian, 22
Thirty-nine Articles, 38
Thomas of Apulia, 26
Thomson, James, 123
Tindal, Matthew, 69-70
Tongues, Gift of, 19, 20-21, 60; *vide* also Gifts of the Spirit

Voltaire, 113

Waldenses, 26
Walpole, Horace, 125
Warburton, William, bishop of Gloucester, 70-71, 127, 134
Warton, Joseph, 117
Watts, Isaac, 134
Wesley, Charles, 57, 123, 146
Wesley, John, in America, 123, 129-130; on asceticism, 122; on church government, 144-145; conversion of, 124; on enthusiasm, 138; on gifts of the Spirit, 136; and Holy Club, 120; preaching of, 125, 135; on scenes at early meetings, 136-137; superstitions of, 138; theology of, 138-144
Westminster Assembly, 39
Westminster Confession, 39
Whichcote, Benjamin, 98-99
Whitefield, George, 129, 134
Whitehead, William, 117-118
Williams, Roger, 65
Winstanley, Gerrard, 104-105
Witchcraft, 89, 99n, 109
Witness of the Spirit, doctrine of, 132, 133-134, esp. 134n, 141
Wyclif, John, 60

Young, Edward, 123

Zwickau, prophets of, 32-33